Fuel

The Most Important Number in your Financial Life

Alok Deshpande

SmartPath Publishing, Atlanta, GA

SmartPath Publishing

Atlanta, GA/30338

info@smartpathfinancial.com

Ordering Information:

Quantity sales. Special discounts are available on quantity purchases by corporations, associations, and others. For details, contact the "Special Sales Department" at the following email – contact@smartpathfinancial.com.

Fuel/Alok Deshpande. —1st ed.

ISBN 978-0-9966611-0-2

This book is dedicated to my mother.

You immigrated to the United States with $8 and became the millionaire next door. This book is inspired by your actions.

Thank you for teaching us how to be smart with money – it's a gift that will impact our family for generations.

Contents

7 Tanks to Fill with Your *Fuel*

Parting Shots

Worksheets

Introduction

Book = 5%, You = 95%

Learn the System

What Gets Tracked, Gets Improved

Focus on What You Can Control

Know Your Why

Book = 5%, You = 95%

Money has been made more complex than necessary.

Most people have the same basic financial goals – own a home, get out of debt, save for retirement, help kids with college, and enjoy life along the way.

Reaching your goals is 95% behavior and 5% strategy and information. This book will give you the 5% (strategy and information) so you can do the 95%.

I figure it's best to lay my cards on the table before you dive into a book that's sole purpose is to help you get on the right track with your money. This book is direct, in your face and unabashed. It teaches a system that has worked for generations and will work for you.

How am I so sure?

- Because, the system is simply common sense with a little structure.

- Because, I've taught the system to thousands of families and seen the results.

- Because the system is based on the rules, not exceptions that make for great media stories and water cooler conversation.

If you're looking for a book that will help you consistently make better financial choices while following a proven plan, you've found it. For get rich quick schemes, complex investing philosophies and, how to lose 50 pounds in one week, visit the front of your local bookstore.

Learn the System

Systems work. Systems give you the strategy so you can focus on execution. They take the guesswork out of making a positive change in your life. Systems such as Weight Watchers, P90X, and countless diet plans have shown amazing results because all you need to do is track your activity and follow the plan.

This book teaches a system. It starts with showing you how to spend less than you make. Then, it gives you 7 goals to reach with that money.

The system works. It's worked for immigrants that barely speak English because it's rooted in basic math. It will also work for you. Learn it, determine where you are in the system, and then focus 100% of your energy on moving forward.

Continue to reference this book as you hit different stages along the journey.

What Gets Tracked, Gets Improved

If you want to succeed in this system, you'll need to track your money. In fact, if you want to improve almost anything in your life, start tracking it. If you're trying to lose weight, get a scale. Want to run faster? You need a stopwatch. Want to drink more water? Count how many times you fill your water bottle. And, if you want to save more money and build wealth, commit to tracking your income and expenses (also known as a budget).

Tracking creates a virtuous cycle. It feeds on our natural desire to improve. When you start tracking something, you begin paying more attention to it. Then, you start to set goals and manage it. Then, you invest more time because you want to see improvement. It's amazing how simply tracking can have an enormous impact on results.

Businesses track sales.

Doctors track your cholesterol.

Attorneys track time.

Students track grades.

If you want to succeed in this system, you'll need to track your money. It may not look good now, but who cares? It will get better. And, you'll know because you're tracking it.

Focus on What You Can Control

You <u>can</u> control how much you spend and make each month.

You *can't* control the return on your investments.

You <u>can</u> control how many hours you clip coupons and search for deals.

You *can't* control which items go on sale.

You <u>can</u> control paying your bills on time and managing the amount of credit you use.

You *can't* control your credit score.

You <u>can</u> control how loud you cheer for your favorite team.

You *can't* control if your team wins a championship.

Focus on what you can control. Be consistent with those actions. Your actions each day will help you work through the system. There will be setbacks that are out of your control (and some that are in your control). Don't get discouraged. Keep executing and results will follow.

Know Your Why

Lastly, before you read another page, know your why. Why are you doing this? Why invest the time, energy and heartache into getting your money right? Sure, it's the "right" thing to do, but that won't sustain you through the tough times.

Working through the system is a marathon. It will feel overwhelming at times. You will hit rough patches. You will get tired of making sacrifices. It will be easy to quit and justify bad financial decisions by saying, "I'm living for today." So, why are you doing this?

Let me propose one reason – **your children** (or future children).

I grew up with parents that intensely saved money. Instead of ordering lemonade, they ordered water, lemons and sugar. To water the plants, they used water from the dehumidifiers. In the summer, the thermostat was set on "blazing" to avoid using the air conditioning. In the winters, we wore thermals instead of using the heater. And, that was only the beginning.

Sure, some people called them "cheap" or "misers." But my parents surrounded themselves with like-minded people. They disregarded the haters. They knew that if they spent less than they made and avoided financial products they didn't understand, good things would happen. Forty years later, they had proof.

First, my parents, who came to the US with little money, became the millionaires next door. They never owned a business. They never hit the lottery. They never made huge profits from investing. Instead, they socked away 30-50 percent of what they made – *every single month.*

Second, my parents instilled positive financial behaviors in my sister and me. We learned by watching them. We watched them make sacrifices. We watched them pass on short term gratification for longer term success. We watched them be creative with how we had fun. And, we were happy. We were very happy.

You have the opportunity to change the direction of your family. You have the power to show (not just tell) your children how to be smart with money. You can lay the groundwork to ensure generations can create and maintain wealth. That's your why.

Now, let's begin our journey by understanding the most important number in your financial life – it's called *Financial Fuel.*

What is *Financial Fuel*?

The Most Important Number in Your Financial Life

Why They Don't Talk About *Fuel*

Meet the Carters

The Most Important Number in Your Financial Life

Financial fuel is the most important number in your financial life. Here's how you calculate it.

Calculation	Example
Your monthly income[1]	$5,000
- Your monthly expenses	-$4,500
= *Your monthly financial fuel*	**$500**

[1] *After taxes, deductions, etc. It's cash that's deposited into your account.*

That's it. *Financial fuel* is the amount of cash you have left each month after you're done spending. It's income minus expenses. It's the money you need to tackle any and every financial goal in your life.

If you want to pay off debt, you need *fuel*. If you want to save for retirement, you need *fuel*. Thinking about buying a house? You'll need *fuel*. Want to send the kids to college? *Fuel*. That yacht on the Mediterranean requires *fuel*. Yes, every financial goal or dream you have needs *fuel*. Without *fuel*, it's impossible to establish a real financial plan.

So why don't you hear more about *fuel*? How can you figure out how much you have? How do you get more *fuel*? And, what should you do with your *fuel*? Keep reading.

Why They Don't Talk About *Fuel*

If *fuel* is so important, why don't you hear more about it? You get plenty of credit card offers. You see countless commercials about investing for retirement. You're bombarded with ads about buying a home so you can achieve the "American Dream." But, you don't see anything about the most basic requirement for any of this – *financial fuel*.

There's a simple reason that no one talks about it. It's because no one makes money from *fuel* except you. Big corporate marketing budgets aren't spent on helping you spend less than you make. Our economy doesn't grow and businesses don't profit by encouraging you to live within your means. *Fuel* is like air – required for life, but rarely discussed.

Don't let the lack of marketing fool you. If you focus on *fuel*, you will be on your way to creating generational wealth. You will pass down money and the ability to keep it. Now, let's figure out how much you have.

Meet the Carters

Meet the Carter family. John is 34 and Tina is 32. They got married four years ago and have a toddler named Willy. They had a beautiful wedding on the beach and, despite Uncle Frank drinking too much, it was a day to remember. Willy has also been a blessing. He's growing fast and recently hit the terrible twos. Life is good.

Now, John and Tina really want (and need) to get their financial life in order. We'll track them through the process.

Tracking Your *Fuel*

How Much *Fuel* Do You Have?

Creating a Living Budget to Track *Fuel*

Ten Happy Days

I Hate the 24th of the Month

I Don't Have *Fuel*

How Much *Fuel* Do You Have?

To begin, you need to figure out how much *fuel* you have each month. Remember, *fuel* is what's left of your income after paying all your monthly expenses. So what's included in income and expenses? Here's a guide:

Income includes . . .

- **Take home pay from your job:** This is the amount of money you bring home from your job. It's the cash that hits your bank account. This is the net amount, after all taxes, insurance deductions, 401(k) deductions, etc. Just add up the checks that hit your account during the month.

- **Extra cash:** Any other cash you get in the month also counts. It could be a tax refund, bonus, child support, what you get for selling an old couch, money from a side hustle, a rebate check, the dollar your co-worker finally paid back, the fifty cents you found between your sofa cushions . . . you get the point. No IOUs. Cash only.

Expenses include . . .

- **Monthly fixed expenses:** This is the amount you pay for your rent or mortgage, utilities, car payment(s), cell phone, pest control, and other items that are the same each month.

- **Monthly discretionary expenses:** This is the amount you pay for food, entertainment, getting your hair and nails done, a beer or three for the football game, and so on.

- **Minimum debt payments:** These are the minimum required payments on your credit cards and other debt. Generally, your statement will show the minimum payment. You may be paying more or want to pay more than the minimum, but, to calculate *fuel*, just use the minimum required payments. Don't worry, you'll pay off your debt as part of the overall system.

That's it. If you automatically pull cash out of your check to save, that's a good habit, but make sure to add it back to calculate *fuel*. *Fuel* is all cash that comes into your account minus all cash that leaves you and goes to someone else.

How much *fuel* did you have last month? The last three months? If you don't know, it's because you haven't been tracking it. You have to track it. We'll get there in a minute.

For now, use your credit card and bank statements to calculate how much *fuel* you had over the last three months. Enter into the worksheet at the back of this book.

John and Tina pulled out their credit card and bank statements to see how much *fuel* they had. Exhibit 1 shows you what they saw. Last month, they spent $345 more than they made. They have negative *financial fuel*. They're not happy.

Exhibit 1: Carter family spending, <u>starting point</u>

INCOME		
Take home pay		
John	$	3,490
Tina	$	2,390
TOTAL TAKE HOME PAY	**$ 5,880**	
EXPENSES		
Housing/car		
Mortgage	$	1,650
Car note (John)	$	350
Utilities		
Electric	$	140
Gas	$	100
Water (occurs every 3 months)	$	50
TV/Internet	$	190
Cellphone	$	180
Insurance		
Auto	$	175
Debt		
Student loans	$	300
Credit cards (minimum payments)	$	100
Other debt minimum payments	$	200
Personal expenses		
Willy's daycare	$	800
Groceries	$	500
Eating out	$	280
Entertainment	$	220
Clothes/shoes	$	165
Tithe	$	300
Gas for the cars	$	350
Medical copays/prescriptions	$	100
Personal items	$	75
TOTAL EXPENSES	**$ 6,225**	
FINANCIAL FUEL	**$ (345)**	

Create a "Living" Budget to Track *Fuel*

If you only calculate your *fuel* at the end of each month, you have no compass. It's the same as checking how much gas you have in your car once a month. At some point you'll find yourself stranded on the side of the road in a place you would rather not be. To avoid that, you generally glance at your gas gauge every time you get in the car. The same should hold true for *financial fuel.*

At any given time, you should know how much money you have left to spend to be on track with *fuel*. There's no point in waiting until the end of the month to see that you've overspent. Track your *fuel* daily and, if you see you're overspending, do something about it.

To track your *fuel*, you'll need to create a "living" budget. On a "living" budget, you enter your expenses every day and make adjustments as you go. Fortunately, there are apps I cover later in this chapter that make this much easier than it sounds.

Here's how you get started...

First, fix a time period for your monthly budget. Your monthly cycle can start on any day of the month – the 1st, 12th, 15th, 19th, 30th . . . it doesn't matter as long as it's an entire month. Hint: You can start this today!

Your budget should have three columns: Budgeted Amount, Actual Amount, and Remaining.

- **Budgeted amount:** In this column, enter your projected income and expenses using our guidelines in the last chapter. Most of these entries should not be guesses. You know how much you'll make this month. You know what your rent and car payments are. You know your debt payments. Don't overcomplicate this. Just put the numbers down.

- **Actual amount:** Every time you spend or make money, make an entry. Manually add it to the "actual amount" column of your budget, or enter it into your app.

  In the beginning, don't automate this. Take the 20 seconds to enter each expense so you're in touch with your money. On average, people have three expenses a day. That's an investment of one minute per day to enter activity into your budget.

- **Remaining:** This is the budgeted amount minus the actual amount. It's what you've got left in that category. If you budgeted $500 for groceries and spent $300, you'd have $200 left. When the "remaining" amount hits $0, you have no money left in that category. While that's frustrating, you now have the data to make a better choice. It could mean eating ramen noodles or you may have money left in other categories. Regardless, knowing the data allows you to make an informed choice.

Take a look at the Carter's budget in Exhibit 2.

Note that despite their past, they've budgeted to have positive $20 of *financial fuel*. It's not much, but it's positive. Don't budget to go deeper into debt! Plan to have at least one dollar of *fuel* (and ideally more). Sure, the month may not turn out the way you planned, but start with a positive goal and work towards reaching it. Use the worksheet at the back of the book to setup a budget for positive *financial fuel*.

There's an App for That

Everyone has a different and unique way of budgeting. Budgets that succeed are more about the person doing the budgeting than the actual method they use. I've known people who budget on napkins and save more than folks using high-tech web tools. Why? It's because their budget is part of their everyday life. They interact with it daily, update it, use it to make decisions, reflect on it, revise it, cuddle with it, and love it. Okay, I may have gone a little too far, but I promise that if you give your budget attention, it will work wonders for you.

That being said, apps are convenient. A few good budgeting apps are GoodBudget (goodbudget.com), You Need A Budget (ynab.com), and Mint (mint.com). On each of them, you can set up your budget, enter expenses as you go, and see what's left. Some apps allow you to connect to your bank account to automate the process. In the beginning, don't automate. It defeats the purpose. It's like trying to automate your workouts. You wouldn't expect to lose weight without doing any pushups, sit-ups, or running. The same holds true with budgeting. You must be involved. When you start this process, manually enter your expenses. Every week, spend fifteen minutes reconciling with your bank and credit card statements to make sure you've entered all your income and expenses. As tracking becomes a habit, you can automate.

Exhibit 2: Carter family budget, <u>beginning of month</u>

	Budgeted	Actual	Remaining
INCOME			
After tax income			
John	$ 3,490	$ -	$ 3,490
Tina	$ 2,390	$ -	$ 2,390
TOTAL TAKE HOME PAY	**$ 5,880**		**$ 5,880**
EXPENSES			
Housing/car			
Mortgage	$ 1,650	$ -	$ 1,650
Car note (John)	$ 350	$ -	$ 350
Utilities			
Electric	$ 130	$ -	$ 130
Gas	$ 90	$ -	$ 90
Water	$ 50	$ -	$ 50
TV/Internet	$ 190	$ -	$ 190
Cellphone	$ 150	$ -	$ 150
Insurance			
Auto	$ 175	$ -	$ 175
Debt			
Student loans	$ 300	$ -	$ 300
Credit cards (min payments)	$ 100	$ -	$ 100
Other debt min payments	$ 200	$ -	$ 200
Personal expenses			
Willy's daycare	$ 800	$ -	$ 800
Groceries	$ 450	$ -	$ 450
Eating out	$ 225	$ -	$ 225
Entertainment	$ 150	$ -	$ 150
Clothes/shoes	$ 125	$ -	$ 125
Tithe	$ 250	$ -	$ 250
Gas for the cars	$ 325	$ -	$ 325
Medical copays/prescriptions	$ 100	$ -	$ 100
Personal items	$ 50	$ -	$ 50
TOTAL EXPENSES	**$ 5,860**	**$ -**	**$ 5,860**
FINANCIAL FUEL	**$ 20**	**$ -**	**$ -**

Ten Happy Days

The first ten days of your budget period are always great. You have money. Nearly every category in your budget shows money remaining.

Exhibit 3 shows John and Tina's budget after the first ten days. They've been good about entering income and expenses. They've been paid and have recorded their deposits. John bought groceries and entered the transactions into the budget. Tina withdrew cash at the ATM and entered it.

Life is good. Every category in their budget shows a positive balance. If they keep this up, they'll have at least $20 of *financial fuel*. This is easy. They're in love. They decide to take a walk along the river and reflect on how great they feel.

Exhibit 3: Carter family budget, <u>after 10 days</u>

	Budgeted	Actual	Remaining
INCOME			
After tax income			
John	$ 3,490	$ 1,745	$ 1,745
Tina	$ 2,390	$ 2,390	$ -
TOTAL TAKE HOME PAY	**$ 5,880**	**$ 4,135**	**$ 1,745**
EXPENSES			
Housing/car			
Mortgage	$ 1,650	$ 1,650	$ -
Car note (John)	$ 350	$ -	$ 350
Utilities			
Electric	$ 130	$ -	$ 130
Gas	$ 90	$ -	$ 90
Water	$ 50	$ 50	$ -
TV/Internet	$ 190	$ 190	$ -
Cellphone	$ 150	$ -	$ 150
Insurance			
Auto	$ 175	$ -	$ 175
Debt			
Student loans	$ 300	$ 300	$ -
Credit cards (min payments)	$ 100	$ -	$ 100
Other debt min payments	$ 200	$ -	$ 200
Personal expenses			
Willy's daycare	$ 800	$ 800	$ -
Groceries	$ 450	$ 175	$ 275
Eating out	$ 225	$ 75	$ 150
Entertainment	$ 150	$ 80	$ 70
Clothes/shoes	$ 125	$ 50	$ 75
Tithe	$ 250	$ 100	$ 150
Gas for the cars	$ 325	$ 125	$ 200
Medical copays/prescriptions	$ 100	$ 50	$ 50
Personal items	$ 50	$ 35	$ 15
TOTAL EXPENSES	**$ 5,860**	**$ 3,680**	**$ 2,180**
FINANCIAL FUEL [1]	**$ 20**	**$ 20**	**$ -**

[1] *Actual financial fuel assumes they will stay on budget in all categories*

I Hate the 24th of the Month

While the early days of your budget period are great, the end of the month is painful. You have no money left. In some categories, you've already gone over. In others, it's just a matter of days. The house is cold because you've turned off the heat. Remember that long walk along the river just a few weeks ago? Feels like a stroll near the septic tank now. By the 24th day of your budget period, you will be tested.

Exhibit 4 shows the Carter family's budget on the 24th of the month.

This sucks. They've already overspent in some categories and the month isn't over. If they stay on this path, they won't have any *fuel*. Now, they have a choice. They can hunker down, stick to the budget, and do everything possible to make sure they have *fuel*, or they can quit.

John and Tina decided to stick it out. Here are a few adjustments they made.

- **Sold stuff:** Yep, they held a garage sale. They'd done everything to cut their expenses to the bone but still were not on track to have *fuel*. Fortunately, they could add some temporary income. They sold a couch, some baby items, a rack of old clothes and added a few hundred dollars of extra cash to their budget.

- **Moved money:** Their electric and gas bills were lower than they'd budgeted. They transferred those savings to groceries to buy some beans, rice, and avocados. John had to have his avocados.

- **Threw a party:** What? I thought they didn't have any money. That's correct. So they held a potluck in the backyard with Willy's friends. Everyone brought food. Tina and John provided the location. They kept the leftovers except one kid's mom who was adamant about taking her remaining pasta salad home with her. Later, they found out she was also building *fuel*!

None of these activities were earth-shattering. John and Tina could have easily quit when things got tough towards the end of the month. It would have been natural. No one would've known or cared. The credit card company would've done the happy dance and maybe sent them more offers. In today's financial world, it's easy to quit because everyone wants you to spend. But, the Carter family didn't. They made it through one month. The next month will be tougher. Game on.

Exhibit 5 shows the Carter family's actual budget at the end of the month. Notice, they went over in some categories (groceries, eating out, clothing), stayed under in others (electric, gas), and made some extra income by selling stuff. In the end, they had $60 of *fuel*. More importantly, they're tracking it. It's a great start.

Exhibit 4: Carter family budget, <u>after 24 days</u>

	Budgeted	Actual	Remaining
INCOME			
After tax income			
John	$ 3,490	$ 3,490	$ -
Tina	$ 2,390	$ 2,390	$ -
TOTAL TAKE HOME PAY	**$ 5,880**	**$ 5,880**	**$ -**
EXPENSES			
Housing/car			
Mortgage	$ 1,650	$ 1,650	$ -
Car note (John)	$ 350	$ 350	$ -
Utilities			
Electric	$ 130	$ 120	$ 10
Gas	$ 90	$ 75	$ 15
Water	$ 50	$ 50	$ -
TV/Internet	$ 190	$ 190	$ -
Cellphone	$ 150	$ 150	$ -
Insurance			
Auto	$ 175	$ 175	$ -
Debt			
Student loans	$ 300	$ 300	$ -
Credit cards (min payments)	$ 100	$ 100	$ -
Other debt min payments	$ 200	$ 200	$ -
Personal expenses			
Willy's daycare	$ 800	$ 800	$ -
Groceries	$ 450	$ 475	$ (25)
Eating out	$ 225	$ 230	$ (5)
Entertainment	$ 150	$ 150	$ -
Clothes/shoes	$ 125	$ 150	$ (25)
Tithe	$ 250	$ 250	$ -
Gas for the cars	$ 325	$ 310	$ 15
Medical copays/prescriptions	$ 100	$ 100	$ -
Personal items	$ 50	$ 50	$ -
TOTAL EXPENSES	**$ 5,860**	**$ 5,875**	**$ (15)**
FINANCIAL FUEL [1]	**$ 20**	**$ 5**	**$ -**

[1] Actual financial fuel is $5 because they are $15 over budget ($20 - $15 = $5)

Exhibit 5: Carter family budget, <u>end of month</u>

	Budgeted	Actual	Remaining
INCOME			
After tax income			
John	$ 3,490	$ 3,490	$ -
Tina	$ 2,390	$ 2,390	$ -
Extra cash			
Selling stuff	$ -	$ 200	$ 200
TOTAL TAKE HOME PAY	**$ 5,880**	**$ 6,080**	**$ 200**
EXPENSES			
Housing/car			
Mortgage	$ 1,650	$ 1,650	$ -
Car note (John)	$ 350	$ 350	$ -
Utilities			
Electric	$ 130	$ 120	$ 10
Gas	$ 90	$ 75	$ 15
Water	$ 50	$ 50	$ -
TV/Internet	$ 190	$ 190	$ -
Cellphone	$ 150	$ 150	$ -
Insurance			
Auto	$ 175	$ 175	$ -
Debt			
Student loans	$ 300	$ 300	$ -
Credit cards (min payments)	$ 100	$ 100	$ -
Other debt min payments	$ 200	$ 200	$ -
Personal expenses			
Willy's daycare	$ 800	$ 800	$ -
Groceries	$ 450	$ 550	$ (100)
Eating out	$ 225	$ 275	$ (50)
Entertainment	$ 150	$ 150	$ -
Clothes/shoes	$ 125	$ 160	$ (35)
Tithe	$ 250	$ 250	$ -
Gas for the cars	$ 325	$ 325	$ -
Medical copays/prescriptions	$ 100	$ 100	$ -
Personal items	$ 50	$ 50	$ -
TOTAL EXPENSES	**$ 5,860**	**$ 6,020**	**$ (160)**
FINANCIAL FUEL[1]	**$ 20**	**$ 60**	**$ -**

[1] *Overbudget by $160 but made an extra $200 so actual fuel was $40 higher*

I Don't Have *Fuel*

Things always turn out great in books. Unfortunately, that's not always true in life. You've tracked your first month and you may not have *fuel*. It's so negative that you don't know where to start.

First, remember this: you're not alone. According to a survey by bankrate.com, 3 out of 4 families are in the same situation.

Second, focus on tracking. What gets tracked gets improved. Tracking gives you data to make better choices. Over time, these choices will lead to more *fuel*.

Third, you now have a single mission. Your mission, should you choose to accept it, is to do everything possible to get more *fuel*. Stop worrying about retirement. Stop arguing about how to pay off debt. Forget about improving your credit score. None of it matters unless you can get more *fuel*. And, there are only two ways to do that — you can either make more or spend less. The next few sections will guide you in both.

Getting More *Fuel*

Making More Money

Tax Refunds, Bonuses and Other Lump Sum Payments

Spend Less

How to Save on Almost Everything

Negotiating

Carter Family – Getting More *Fuel*

Making More Money

To get more *fuel*, you can either make more or spend less. Spending less has limits as we all have basic necessities. Making more, however, is unlimited if you're willing to put in the work. So, how do you do that?

There is no single way to make money. You're most consistent income will come from your job. Don't let that go. But here are several ways to add to your income.

- **Sell your talent:** The Internet has changed the world. If you're looking for options to get paid, it's created opportunities. Online companies such as Upwork.com, ELance.com, and Fiverr.com have created a marketplace for your skills. These sites have contract opportunities for administrative support, writing, web development, software development, customer service, design, and the list goes on. Take the time to upload your profile and apply for side jobs.

- **Sell a service with minimal expenses:** Let me start by saying, this is not about becoming the next Apple. Instead, it's about making money. Identify services that can provide immediate income with limited expenses like babysitting, catering, yard service, running errands, etc. Set a target for the number of clients you need and spend as little as possible to get there. You can even use apps like ShakeLaw.com to handle any legal contracts.

  For example, you may need ten catering clients to make $1,000/month. Focus on getting the first client, then the next, and then the next. Make some small investments in a starter website ($250), 500 business cards ($50), and a Facebook/Twitter presence. Avoid temptations to invest more until you reach your ten clients. Then, you can focus on getting to twenty clients. Spend 1% of your time dreaming and 99% of your time making it happen.

- **Sell your time:** We're living in a 'shared' economy. You can profit from it. Look into contract work with services like Uber.com (ride sharing), Zirtual.com (virtual assistants), TaskRabbit.com (assistants) and InstaEDU.com (tutoring). Every month, new services that need contractors pop up. Don't get fixated on how much (or little) they pay. Instead, focus on how a few hours a week can work wonders on your *fuel*.

- **Find an internship:** Small businesses (and even some larger ones) try to stay as lean as possible, but always need extra resources. Internships can get your foot in the door and keep your skills in top shape. Send handwritten letters to companies in your industry. Use sites such as data.com and linkedin.com to identify and contact the right person at the companies that interest you.

- **Volunteer:** Huh? How do you make money volunteering? You're right, you don't. But, by volunteering, you can show the world that you're a hard worker and care about the community. Volunteering showcases your character and commitment more than a résumé ever could. And, if you volunteer your specific skills (e.g., bookkeeping, legal support, etc.), you stay current while meeting people that may have access to jobs. Volunteering is personally and professionally rewarding and will lead to making money. Check out volunteermatch.org and idealist.org to get started.

- **Sell something:** You could look through your house or apartment today and find enough stuff to have a small garage sale. Fortunately, with online market-places such as craigslist.com, ebay.com and Facebook, all you need is an Internet connection to start selling. In fact, the Internet has even made it easy to rent your entire house (airbnb.com) or car (relayrides.com) when you're not using them.

  Everything you own (yes, everything) has value to someone, and online selling makes the world your marketplace. Still, it takes hard work, persistence, and creativity to stand out from the crowd. Here are a few tips on selling just about anything:

  - *Price on value, not emotion:* Most items you sell will have little-to-no value to you. That's why they are in a box under another box in the corner of the attic. Be willing to set a price that sells the item as fast as possible. Remember, you're trying to add to your *fuel*, not *fuel* your ego.

  - *Find out what sells:* I once met a woman who spent six months on eBay figuring out what people buy. Then, she spent one Saturday a month at garage sales buying those items. After one year, she was making $3,000 a month profit from buying and selling stuff online. That was $3,000 a month in addition to her full-time job. A little research and persistence can go a long way.

- ○ *Automate whenever possible:* If you're selling online, there will be tons of emails and messages. Try to develop a few standard replies to frequently asked questions (FAQs) to avoid constantly typing new messages. It will save you time and frustration. Inexpensive email marketing tools like mailchimp.com and aweber.com can help you automate and save time.

- **Search for a job:** If you don't have a job, dislike your current job, or feel significantly underpaid, I assume you're searching for a job. While this book isn't about how to get a job, a steady source of income is critical to having *fuel.* Here are a few tips for your job search:

  - ○ *Focus on what you can control:* Apply, network, and stay current. That's all you can do. Send as many applications and/or follow-up notes as possible every week. Set up one or two meetings a week for networking (not asking for a job). Read four to six hours a week about topics in your industry. Maximize what you can control and be patient. Your time is coming.

  - ○ *Swallow your pride:* If you have a steady source of income, you can hold on to some of your pride. If you don't have any income, pride should be the last of your concerns. Instead of holding out for the job that you want, find the job that wants you. Once you have a steady source of income, you can look to upgrade.

Does this seem overwhelming? It doesn't have to. Pick one option and get started. Be patient with the process – it will take at least a month to see results.

Tax Refunds, Bonuses, and Other Lump-Sum Payments

It feels good to get a tax refund. You may think your problems are solved. They're not. Most people spend their refund before the cash even hits the bank. In December, they will say, "I'll get my refund in March, and this year I'm claiming my other daughter, so count me in for that vacation!"

Before they know it, they've spent the entire tax refund and then some.

Instead, the first trick to being smart with a pending big check is to wait until you have it. Then, follow the 10/20/70 rule. Here's how the rule works with a $1,000 tax refund:

- **10% ($100)**: Spend 10% of it. Get what you want. Get it now. Enjoy it.

- **20% ($200)**: Put it aside as a reward. It's a reward when you complete your current goal (also known as a 'tank') in the 7-Tank System[1]. If you're filling your 1-month emergency fund, you'll get $200 to spend when you finish. It's a little extra motivation.

- **70% ($700)**: Put this towards the tank you're currently filling in the 7-Tank System. Don't try to divide this money and apply it to different tanks such as paying off debt, building an emergency fund, investing, etc. That doesn't work.

---

[1] As a reminder, the 7-Tank System walks you through the steps (also known as tanks) you will fill with your *financial fuel*. We will cover each 'tank' in detail in the next section.

Instead, figure out which tank you're filling in the System and put all 70% towards filling that tank. If you don't have a one-month emergency fund, fill that. If you have a one-month fund but still have bad debt, use it to pay debt. If you're past bad debt, fill your emergency fund with three to six months' of cushion. And, if you're past all of that, fill your retirement.

You may be asking - what about a down payment on a house? What about investing in a business? If you're past tank #4 (a 3-6 month emergency fund), you can consider these options with your 70%. If not, stick with the plan. A few more big checks and you'll be in great shape.

Spend Less

In addition to making more, you need to spend less. Yes, it's hard. Fortunately, you don't need to make it happen all at once. Spending less should be done in a way that doesn't make your life miserable.

Before we get into specific savings tips, consider the following truths on spending less:

- **You can reduce any expense:** Even the expenses you believe are fixed can be changed over time. Some expenses take more time than others (i.e., rent or a car loan may take longer to change), but every expense can be reduced.

- **Small cuts matter:** It's difficult to find big cuts in your budget. Instead, you need to find small cuts in as many categories as possible. Nickels and dimes will help you build *financial fuel*. The more nickels and dimes you find, the more *fuel* you'll get.

- **How much is more important than what (aka prioritize):** What you spend on is irrelevant. How much you spend is all that matters. We all have different values. Fortunately, *fuel* doesn't judge your values. It does, however, judge how much you spend on your values each month.

  Let's assume you need to keep your total expenses to $3,500 a month to have positive *financial fuel*. If you have an $800 car note, that's okay, but you may not have money left to eat out. If, on the other hand, you eat out two or three times a week, your car likely needs to be paid off to stay below $3,500.

When you focus on *fuel*, how much you spend is more important than what you buy. So, instead of trying to change your values, prioritize aggressively. Enjoy the items you want but cut back on the items where you're indifferent.

- **Budgets evolve over time:** Your budget this month may be different than next month. This year's budget will look different than next year's. You may need to cut entertainment expenses in the near term, but you'll get them back once you pay off debt or add extra income. Life changes. So does your budget. Focus on getting *financial fuel* every month and the rest will take care of itself.

How to Save on Almost Everything

You didn't think I would just leave you with some great philosophical points on saving, did you? Here are some more specific savings tips on common expenses:

Groceries

It's all about unit price. Unit price is shown in ratios such as "$/oz" or "$/lb." Every item has a unit price and your goal is to get the lowest unit price without sacrificing quality. For example, if you're buying sugar, find the lowest price per ounce (unit price) for the amount you need. Here are some ways to get a low unit price:

- **Coupons:** You can save a ton if you use coupons on the items you already buy. Again, coupons only work if you use them on <u>items you already buy</u>. Some great grocery coupon sites include:

  - couponmom.com
  - smartsource.com
  - coupons.com
  - redplum.com
  - iheartkroger.com or iheartpublix.com
  - southernsavers.com
  - hip2save.com

- **Store brand:** Store brands (aka private label) is generally cheaper than their branded counterparts. Look at the nutrition labels to make sure you're buying the equivalent product.

- **Farmers' markets:** Many cities have local farmers' markets where prices can be 20-50% lower on meats and vegetables. Take a trip to your local farmers' market.

- **Bulk shopping:** When you buy in bulk, the unit price is generally lower. Costco, Sam's Club, and many online outlets have great prices if you're buying in bulk. Be careful not to buy more than you need. If you throw stuff away, you're not truly saving. Instead, you're throwing away money.

Be patient. It will take a few hours to learn how these options can save you money. Once you figure out what works for you, you'll see the difference in your budget and *fuel*.

Eating Out

It's always nice to treat yourself by eating out but, how nice? Is it worth it? Here are some good ways to save on eating out:

- **Do it less:** The easiest way to save on eating out is by doing it less. Bring your lunch to work. Have fewer Starbucks lattes. Get creative on your dates. It's easier said than done, but it's still possible. Remember, *financial fuel* rules.

- **Savings sites:** Groupon.com, LivingSocial.com, and nCrowd.com are a few of the hundreds of new websites that give great deals on restaurants and other entertainment. Find the ones you like and use them. Don't buy items that are not in your budget. If you see yourself buying a half-off helicopter tour of the city, it's probably time to stop.

- **Doggie bag:** Restaurants often serve too much food. When your food comes, ask the waiter to put half in a to-go box. Now you have lunch for tomorrow.

Electric Bill

Your bill is calculated by multiplying usage times rate (usage x rate). You might be able to get a better rate by shopping around and/or cutting your usage. Here are some tips to reduce your electric bill:

- **Seal it up:** Close your blinds and make sure all entryways are sealed against drafts. Make sure you have proper insulation in your attic and walls. Make the most of what you have.

- **Fans:** Turn them on. At the same time, turn down the air conditioning. Changing your thermostat a few degrees can lead to serious savings in the summer.

- **Unplug:** Most electrical appliances use electricity when they're plugged in, even when they're not being used. Unplug appliances and electronics when you're not using them.

- **Fix your bill:** This tip is less about saving and more about transparency. It's easier to budget if you know your expenses. Fixed bills, sometimes called level payments, will spread your average usage throughout the year so you pay the same amount every month. Of course, the utility company will still track usage, so be careful and focus on using less.

- **Shop around:** If you live in an unregulated state, you have options. Shop around and don't be afraid to switch suppliers or, at least, tell your power company that you have better options. They will negotiate rather than lose you as a customer.

- **High Efficiency appliances:** I'm torn about these. It's true, high-efficiency appliances do help you save. At the same time, it's not worth using a credit card or raiding your emergency fund to buy a high-efficiency appliance. If it's time for a new appliance, high-efficiency may be the way to go. Otherwise, wait until it's time.

Gas Bill

Just like the electric bill, your gas bill is calculated by multiplying usage times rate (usage x rate). The less you use or the better rate you have, the less you spend. Here are some tips to reducing your gas bill:

- **Seal up:** If gas heats your house, then similar to electric, you need insulation. Make sure your attic, walls, ducts, and pipes have some level of insulation. If they don't, save up to get it done and it will pay off over time.

- **Clothes:** As a child, I remember wearing sweatshirts, socks, and sometimes even thermal underwear in the house. It worked. I'm fine, and my parents saved a ton by keeping the heat off.

- **Vents:** Don't heat rooms that you don't use. Shut the vents. You'll feel the difference in your bill.

- **Fix your rate:** You can usually choose between variable and fixed rates. A fixed rate helps you avoid the ups and downs in natural gas prices. Generally, you can lock in a great per therm rate for six to twelve months. Do it. Consistency is good.

- **Fix your bill:** Same as in the case of your electric bill, fixed bills (or level payments) help you avoid surprises and stay on track with your budget.

- **Shop around:** Depending on where you live, you may have tons of options with your gas service. A simple Google search can help you identify the different providers in your area and their current rates. Pick up the phone, call each provider, and make sure you're getting the best rate.

Cell Phone

What do you really use? It seems like everyone wants the Cadillac of cellphone plans, but then they spend 95% of their time on talk and text. Here are some ways to lower your cell phone bill:

- **Select the right plan:** Avoid overages. Look at your minutes for the past three months and find a plan that fits. If you're going over your minutes, upgrade or talk less.

- **Use WiFi:** Data plans can hurt, and overages can kill you. Use WiFi and turn off cellular data wherever possible—especially at home.

- **Align with usage:** Monitor what you use. If you're paying for features you don't use, turn them off. It sounds simple, but most people don't bother.

- **Avoid extras:** Avoid getting roadside assistance, streaming videos, and other "cool" features that you never use. Even if it's only $2.95/month, it adds up. If you don't use it every month, it's not worth it.

- **Think "worst case":** Cellphone promotions change. The phone companies want to give you ways to have what you want, not necessarily what you need. When you evaluate a promotion, focus on the worst case scenario. For example, if there's a monthly payment option on a phone, understand what it would cost if you lost or damaged the phone in the first few months. Is it still worth it? Would it be smarter to get a subsidized phone and sign a contract? If it looks too good to be true, it probably is.

Clothes/Stuff

What about other purchases such as kids' shoes, clothes, household items, and the rest? These expenses make up a much larger portion of your budget than you think. Here are some ways to save:

- **Google images:** You can find coupons for just about any major store using Google images. Let's say I want to go to Sports Authority for new running shoes. I go to images.google.com and type "Sports Authority printable coupons". A number of Sports Authority coupons will appear. Go through them and see which ones apply. You can follow the same process for other large retailers that offer coupons.

- **Off season:** Buy winter clothes in the spring. Buy summer clothes in the fall. Everything will be on clearance. When retailers are desperately trying to get rid of inventory, you'll benefit.

- **Outlets:** Outlets can offer good deals, assuming you don't overspend. Outlet malls are generally located a few hours outside of major cities. The drive makes people feel like they need to buy more to make the trip worthwhile. If you've saved for the trip, great. If not, you're better off at Walmart, Target, and other discount department stores.

- **Used:** Consignments stores, craigslist.com, and ebay.com are great for buying used goods. Consider used toys, cars, electronics, sporting goods, books, art, and household items. Don't buy used underwear, sports apparel, or food (at least I wouldn't).

I've only scratched the surface of ways to save on just about anything. Once you've tasted success by finding a killer deal, you'll be hooked. But, be careful. If you're buying items that are not in your budget, you're not truly saving.

Negotiating

Whether it's to make more or spend less, negotiate everything. You will succeed less than 10% of the time. They will say 'no' 90% of the time. Still, practice makes perfect. I've negotiated at restaurants, grocery stores, electronics stores, and even Walmart. I enjoy the discussion. I enjoy the process of finding a deal where both parties win. Don't be afraid to simply ask. Just make sure you're prepared. Here are a few tips to get started:

- **It's not only about the price:** If your goal is to simply ask for a price discount, expect rejection 99.9% of the time. Price is the most difficult negotiating item. It instantly creates a win-lose situation. Instead, be creative.

  - o Ask for a free dessert at a restaurant in exchange for thoughtfully completing a comment card.

  - o Ask for free guest passes before joining your local gym.

  - o Ask for 20% off the floor model or open box item (as-is) if you buy a few more things.

- **Win/win:** Negotiating is not a hustle. You're not trying to beat the other person. Negotiating is about figuring out what the salesperson or business needs, and offering that in exchange for something you need. Both parties should win. No one likes to lose. Both parties should feel good after the deal.

For example, salespeople at large electronics stores are often paid higher commissions on selling extended warranties. If you're buying a TV, ask them to reduce the price of the set and you'll buy the full-price extended warranty. They get a higher commission and you get a free warranty. Both parties win.

- **Discuss multiple items:** When buying a car, consider price, features, financing options, color, and interior as part of the negotiation. Maybe the dealership can lower the price if you finance with them. Maybe they have too many black cars and they're willing to add a navigation system if you take one. They won't tell you what they need. You will find out by discussing multiple items at the same time.

- **BATNA:** BATNA is your Best Alternative To a Negotiated Agreement. You need to know your BATNA. What's your next best alternative if you don't get the deal you want? If you don't have an alternative, keep that to yourself. If you have an alternative, share it wisely with the salesperson. For example, call competing cable/Internet providers to get their best offers. Ask your current cable company if they will match. If not, you don't need to switch, but at least you tried to lower your costs.

- **Grounding:** Make an offer. Make the first offer. Don't ask, "Can I get a discount?" No one wants to simply give a discount. Instead, try to ask, "I can pay $300 for that TV and use either cash or credit. Which one would you prefer?" By getting the first offer out, you ground the discussion. You let the salesperson know you're willing to buy and it sets an opening position. Now, they must react with a yes, no, or counteroffer. It starts the discussion on your terms and increases your chances of success.

- **No emotion:** If you can't live without the product, you can't negotiate. You must be willing to walk away. You can't show emotion or urgency when you're buying. Make it feel like an impulse purchase – you're simply browsing and you noticed the product. If it's a service, the same holds true. You're interested, but willing to walk away. In other words, don't take your children to the store. They kill all negotiating leverage.

- **Listen:** Uncomfortable silence is awesome. You want the other party to talk more. You want information. You want to know their needs and what's important to them. You want to know what motivates them. You want to fully understand their counteroffer. But, you won't get any of this if you're doing all the talking. Listen and allow for uncomfortable silences. The other party will tell you what you need to know to make a win-win deal.

- **Prepare:** Don't wing it. Have a plan before starting the discussion. Know your different options and what you want. Write them down. Think through the rebuttals. Practice with a friend. The negotiation will go much more smoothly.

Negotiating is an art, not a science. Practice in situations where you know you'll be rejected. Get comfortable with the feeling of someone saying 'no'. Hone your skills. Find out what works for you. Repeat. Save more. Make more. Get more *financial fuel*.

⊙ Carter Family - Getting More *Fuel*

As you may recall, John and Tina Carter were not happy about not having any *fuel*. At first, they argued about whose fault it was. They questioned each other's purchases. They whined and nagged to the point where two-year-old Willy had to intervene. When he did, they realized the past is the past and started to get on track.

After a few difficult months, exhibit 6 shows you their revised budget. They went from overspending by $345 each month to a positive $320 of *fuel*! Notice, their life was not turned completely upside down. Instead, they made some small, conscious changes. More importantly, they committed to tracking their budget in an app. By doing so, they can see how they're doing in real time and stay on track.

The same is possible for you. Commit to tracking for one day, then two, then a week and then a month. It will become a habit and you will have *fuel*.

Use the worksheet at the back of the book to enter a few ideas of how you can make more and spend less. Then, start working on one idea in each.

Now, let's discuss what you do with your newfound *fuel*.

Exhibit 6: Carter family budget, revised

	Original	Revised
INCOME		
After tax income		
John	$ 3,490	$ 3,490
Tina	$ 2,390	$ 2,390
Extra cash		
Some type of extra income	$ -	$ 150
TOTAL TAKE HOME PAY	$ 5,880	$ 6,030
EXPENSES		
Housing/car		
Mortgage	$ 1,650	$ 1,650
Car note (John)	$ 350	$ 350
Utilities		
Electric	$ 140	$ 130
Gas	$ 100	$ 90
Water	$ 50	$ 50
TV/Internet	$ 190	$ 190
Cellphone	$ 180	$ 140
Insurance		
Auto	$ 175	$ 175
Debt		
Student loans	$ 300	$ 300
Credit cards (min payments)	$ 100	$ 100
Other debt min payments	$ 200	$ 200
Personal expenses		
Willy's daycare	$ 800	$ 800
Groceries	$ 500	$ 450
Eating out	$ 280	$ 215
Entertainment	$ 220	$ 110
Clothes/shoes	$ 165	$ 110
Tithe	$ 300	$ 200
Gas for the cars	$ 350	$ 300
Medical copays/prescriptions	$ 100	$ 100
Personal items	$ 75	$ 50
TOTAL EXPENSES	$ 6,225	$ 5,710
FINANCIAL FUEL	$ (345)	$ 320

7 Tanks to Fill with Your *Fuel*

Overview of the 7-Tank System

#1 - Company Match for Retirement

#2 - 1-Month Emergency Fund

#3 - Bad Debt Free

#4 - Emergency Fund to Cover 3-6 Months

#5 - 20% of Gross Income to Retirement

#6 - Children's College

#7 - Bucket List

Summary of the 7-Tank System

Overview of the 7-Tank System

You're tracking your money every day. You're starting to have positive *financial fuel* every month. You're making adjustments as you go. You're in control. Congratulations! You've conquered the hardest part of managing your money.

Now, what do you do with your newfound monthly *fuel*? Fill the following 7 tanks in this order. Skip the ones that don't apply.

The 7-Tank System

#1 - Company Match for Retirement

#2 - 1-Month Emergency Fund

#3 - Bad Debt Free

#4 - Emergency Fund to cover 3-6 Months

#5 - 20% of Gross Income to Retirement

#6 - Children's College

#7 - Bucket List

Again, fill these tanks in order. The order works. If your company has a retirement matching program, make sure you contribute up to the match. Then, if you don't have a 1-month emergency fund, focus on filling that. If you have a 1-month fund but still have bad debt, direct your *fuel* to paying it off.

Don't try to fill all the tanks at once. Figure out which tank you're filling and get focused. All your *fuel* should go to that tank until it's full (or finished). Then, move to the next.

Filling each tank will take time. In fact, you can calculate exactly how much time it will take. For example:

- If your 1-month emergency fund requires $3,000 and you're adding $300 of *fuel* each month, it will take you 10 months to fill that tank.

- If you can increase your *fuel* to $600 a month, it will take half the time (5 months).

- If your *fuel* drops to $150 a month, it will take you twice as long (20 months).

By focusing on *fuel*, you're in complete control. The more *fuel* you have, the faster you'll fill the tanks. If you have less *fuel*, you'll go slower.

The next few sections will give you more details and direction on each tank. In each section, we'll track the Carter family as an example. Remember, their revised budget will give them $320 of *fuel* each month. Let's see how they fill their 7 tanks.

Note
Use the worksheets in the back of the book to help you get organized, run calculations and understand which tank you must fill next. Remember, reading this book is only the first step. The worksheets will help you take action!

#1 - Company Match for Retirement

Your company's retirement matching program gives you free money as long as you participate. It's an incentive for you to save. The amount and rules may vary, but it's still free money if you do your part.

There are two parts to your retirement matching program – the match and the vesting schedule.

Part 1: The Match

With a match, your company will add money to your retirement account if you put your own money in first. Here's how it works:

- Let's say your company matches 50% of the first 6% you contribute.

- You contribute 6% of your paycheck to your retirement account *(This is typically done online through the company that handles your retirement plan. Ask HR if you need help).*

- Your employer will contribute an additional 3% of their money to your retirement account *(They contribute an additional 50% of your 6%, which is 3%).*

- In total, you retirement account will get 9%. 6% will come from your paycheck and 3% will come from your employer's match.

- Continue every month. Keep getting free money.

If you don't contribute, your employer doesn't contribute. It's that simple. Your retirement matching program is a benefit from your employer. They want you to save for your retirement and are willing to help if you help yourself.

Part 2: Vesting Schedule
The second part of the matching program is the vesting schedule. Vesting tells you when the money your employer contributes is actually yours. Companies use vesting schedules to retain employees. Here's how it works with the above example:

- The 6% you contributed is 100% vested – it's all yours at the moment you contribute and is now in your retirement savings account.

- The 3% your employer contributed is on a vesting schedule that is either immediate, graded, or cliff.

  o If it's immediate vesting, the 3% they contribute is all yours, immediately.

  o If it's graded vesting, you get the 3% <u>over</u> a certain period of time. For example, if it's 4-year graded, you get ownership of a quarter of their contribution each year for the first four years. After four years, it's all yours, for all future years.

  o If it's cliff vesting, you get the 3% <u>after</u> a certain period of time. For example, if it's 4-year cliff, you get everything they've contributed after you've completed four years of service. During the four years, the company puts their match in a side account and then gives you a lump sum at the end of four years.

If vesting is still a little hazy, don't worry about it. You should contribute to the matching program regardless of the vesting schedule. All vesting means is that, if you leave your employer before the end of the vesting, you may be leaving some of their match behind. Don't focus on that. Instead, focus on getting as much free money as you can. Contribute to the match.

Now, I know what you're thinking,

"If I contribute to my retirement, my paycheck will be smaller."

You're right. So let me show you the trade-off for that small sacrifice.

Let's use the Carter family as an example.

Tina's employer doesn't match, so she can skip this tank.

- John's employer matches 50% up to the first 5%.

- John makes $55,000 per year, or $4,583 per month before taxes.

- If John contributes 5%, he will contribute $230/month ($4,583 x 5% = $230).

- His employer will make a contribution equal to half of John's contribution, which is $115/month (Half of $230 is $115).

- John is in the 25% tax bracket.

- Since his retirement contribution is pre-tax money, his check will be smaller by about $170/month ($230 x (1-25%) =~$170).

So, John's monthly check will be ~$170 less. If he has *fuel*, it will be reduced since his take home pay will be smaller. If not, he will need to cut his monthly expenses by $170 to make room. In return, he gets an additional $115 from his employer each month.

So how much will that $115 per month be worth when John retires in 30 years?

$95,700[2]

Bling, Bling! Amazing, huh? John gets an extra $95,700 from his employer by simply contributing to the matching program. This $95,700 is in addition to his own contributions. It's big money. It's free money. If you're living paycheck to paycheck, it may take a few months to get to a point where you can contribute, but getting the match should be your first priority.

Note

In the 7-Tank System, you'll fill your retirement in tank #1 and #5. For tank #1, you should contribute up to the match to get the free money. Then, in tank #5, you increase your retirement contribution to 20% of gross pay. Don't worry, it will make sense as you go through the system. To fill tank #1, contribute up to the match to get all the free money you can.

---

[2] Assumes $115 per month for 30 years at 5% annual growth, compounded monthly.

⊚ Carter Family: #1 - Company Match for Retirement

John's employer matches up to 5%. He should begin by contributing 5%. Tina's employer doesn't match. She should not contribute until she's filling tank #5.

Here's John and Tina's *fuel* before and after contributing to the match for tank #1:

	Before	After
John income[1]	$3,490	$3,320
Tina income	$2,390	$2,390
Extra income	$150	$150
Total income	$6,030	$5,860
- Expenses	-$5,710	-$5,710
= Financial Fuel	**$320**	**$150**

[1] *John's check was $170 less because he contributed to the match*

Notice, contributing up to the match lowered John's take home pay and, as a result, lowered their *fuel*. It's okay. John is contributing to his retirement and taking advantage of the free additional contributions from his employer. Nice work.

#2 - 1-Month Emergency Fund

After contributing to the retirement match, it's time to build a small emergency fund. You'll need *fuel*. If you don't have any, go back to the section on "Getting More *Fuel*."

Here's an overview of the 1-Month Emergency Fund:

How much is it?

It's the amount you would need to last one month if you lost your job. We'll increase this to 3-6 months when filling tank #4. But, to fill tank #2, you need to save enough to cover one month of core expenses. Core expenses include rent/mortgage, low utilities, minimum debt payments, insurance, medical costs, low food/gas and basic cell phone. It does not include cable, eating out, clothes, your expensive data plan, etc. Remember, you're trying to figure out how much you need for one month if you lost your job. All extras would go out the door.

The amount does not need to be exact. Estimate how much you need and go with it.

Where do I invest it?

You don't invest it. Your 1-month emergency fund should be accessible. You can keep it in your checking account or a small savings account. Don't invest it. This is not savings for your future. It's simply an emergency fund for when life happens.

When do I use it?

You use it when you have an emergency. You will get a flat tire. Your roof will spring a leak. You will need to bail someone out of jail. You will have emergencies (or bad luck) throughout your life. If you don't have an emergency fund, you'll use a credit card or other debt. That's not good.

By the way, a new pair of shoes for a wedding is not an emergency. Neither is going out for drinks to catch the NBA Finals. Those are either part of your budget or it's time to get creative.

What do I do after I use it?

If you use money from your emergency fund, replenish it. If you use $200 from your fund, put it back before moving on with your plan. You will need to fill this tank a few times during the process. Eventually, you'll have enough saved that you'll never touch this 1-Month Emergency Fund.

Why am I doing this before paying off my credit cards?

You're building this fund first to avoid the Credit Card Vicious Cycle of Charges Death Trap (aka CCVCCDT). Yes, it's as bad as it sounds. It's an epidemic in the United States. Emergencies with no emergency fund equal more charges. More charges leads to more interest. More interest leads to a deeper hole of debt. It happens to the best of us.

Imagine spending six months paying down your credit cards. You're feeling good. Then, your car's alternator goes out, and you need $400 for repairs. If you don't have an emergency fund, you charge it. Then, your debt goes right back up. It's frustrating. It's demoralizing. It's demotivating. And, worst of all, there's little you can do.

An emergency fund protects you from CCVCCDT. It gives you a foundation so, when you start paying off bad debt, you don't have setbacks.

⊙ Carter Family: #2 - 1-Month Emergency Fund

The Carter family decides they need $3,000 to get through one month without jobs. So, to fill tank #2, they need $3,000. First, they check their savings. They have $600 already saved. Therefore, they need another $2,400 to have a 1-month emergency fund and fill tank #2.

After setting up their monthly contributions to John's retirement match, the Carter family has $150 of *financial fuel* each month. To reach $2,400, it will take them 16 months ($2,400/$150 = 16).

Now, they have a choice.

If they want to fill faster, they can increase their *fuel* by adding income or cutting expenses. For example, if they increase their *fuel* to $250 per month, they will fill tank #2 in less than 10 months.

On the flip side, if their *fuel* drops below $150, it will take longer. For example, if their monthly *fuel* drops to $100 per month, it will tank them 24 months to fill tank #2.

It's their choice. John and Tina are in control.

#3 - Bad Debt Free

Debt sucks. It piles up over time. It started before you knew what it was. It's frustrating. It's not your fault. Well, maybe it's a little your fault. It doesn't matter. It's in the past. But remember this feeling. You don't want to have this feeling again.

With your 1-month emergency fund, you've protected yourself from adding to your debt. That's comforting. Now it's time to get free of bad debt. But which ones should you pay off? What's the right order? Is it okay to just make payments on any of your debt? Tank #3 will give you a guide.

In tank #3, you will pay off bad debt while making payments on the not-so-bad debt. This is a balanced approach. This approach allows you to enjoy today and get on track for your future. I know some advisors suggest you pay off all your debt. I don't. I don't think it's realistic. It leads to burnout and relapse. Instead, in tank #3, you use your *fuel* to pay off the debt that will drown you while making payments on debt that's manageable[3].

---

[3] Adapt this plan to your situation. If you have not-so-bad debts with uncomfortably high balances or interest rates, treat them like bad debt. Remember, you will ultimately pay it all off.

Here are the two types of debt:

Bad Debt – Pay these off to complete tank #3

- Mob debt
- Payday loans, Title loans and other super high interest debt
- Credit cards
- Private student loans
- Medical debt
- Tax debt
- Retirement plan loan

Not-so-Bad Debt – Keep making payments until tank #7

- Federal student loans
- Auto loans
- Mortgage
- Home equity

First, let's take a look at each of the bad debts.

Bad Debt

To complete tank #3, pay off all the debts in this section.

Mob Debt

There are some people you should never borrow from. They include people who will cause bodily harm, nosy family members, and that person who will never leave you alone. It's called mob debt, and you should pay it first. Mob debt creditors do not use a collections agency. Instead, its debt to people you know. It's debt to people that will, in some way, always be in your life. It's debt that makes you uncomfortable and alters relationships. It's debt that eats at you every day. You know you have mob debt when...

- You can't wear new clothes around this person because they will ask you where you got the money.

- You can't invite this person over to your house because they believe they're entitled to anything of yours until you pay them back.

- You can't discuss money in front of this person because they will tell everyone that you owe them.

They're not bad people. They're simply people to whom you don't want to owe money. If you have mob debt, pay it.

Payday Loans, Title Loans, and Other Super-High Interest Debt

According to the Center for Responsible Lending, the average interest rate on a payday loan is 400%. Interest rates on title loans and pawn lending can exceed 200%. Refund anticipation loans and Buy Here Pay Here auto loans carry interest rates well above 50%. If you rent-to-own, you pay three times as much for the item. Check cashing costs 7-10% of your check. All of these services are ridiculous. They ruin your chance at financial freedom. They give you hope in a time of desperation and then take it away when you realize how long and how much you will pay.

I know, there are times when you think you have no other choice. You'll only do it once to get out of a jam. I don't buy it. Eight out of ten people keep taking these loans to pay the old loan. It's a trap. You're caught.

If you're in the market for these types of services, here are a few alternatives to consider:

- **Credit unions / Community banks:** They cash checks. They are nonprofits with a mission to help you. Go to your local credit union. Find out how to open an account. They may have fees but they're small in comparison to check cashing.

- **Walmart:** I don't like the idea of check cashing, but if you're doing it, Walmart has the lowest prices. It's $3 for up to a $1,000 check and $6 for up to a $5,000 check. Not great, but much better than the alternatives.

- **Don't buy it:** This is easier said than done. If it's life-threatening, a payday loan is the least of your worries. Most purchases are not life-threatening. You don't need furniture in every room. You don't need a big screen TV. You don't need to go out tonight. Get out of the cycle. Revisit your *financial fuel*. You'll have more fun in the long run.

If you've already taken the plunge into one of these loans, get out fast. Stop reading this book, find every penny you have and pay them off. These loans keep you broke. They're predatory. They hurt you and make you dependent. You're better off smoking.

Credit Cards

There are hundreds of books and blogs that highlight the dangers of credit cards. You don't need to read the fine print to understand credit cards. Card companies (banks) make money by charging you interest. They want to charge you as much interest as possible so they can make as much money as possible. In return, they give you the freedom to buy things you can't afford. And, to sweeten the deal, they give you rewards and discounts that are never worth as much as you pay in interest. It's crazy. The entire credit system is insane, but that's another story.

There are two strategies to pay off your credit card debt. Let's use the Carter family as an example to show each strategy.

Carter family credit card debt

Card Name	Outstanding Balance	Interest Rate
VISA	$800	22.50%
AMEX	$2,200	29.90%
Home Depot	$450	12.90%
Target	$550	8.90%
Total	**$4,000**	

Strategy 1: Pay off highest interest rate first

In this strategy, John and Tina would pay off the highest interest rate card first, the AMEX. While they're paying off the AMEX, they'll make minimum payments on the other cards. Once they're done with the AMEX, they'll move to the next highest rate card, the VISA. They'll keep going through this process, paying off cards in descending order of their interest rates.

This strategy saves money. John and Tina will pay the least total interest by paying the card with the highest rate first.

Strategy 2: Pay off lowest balance first

In this strategy, John and Tina would pay off the lowest balance card first, the Home Depot card. While they're paying off the Home Depot card, they'll make minimum payments on the other cards. Once they're done with the Home Depot card, they'll move to the next lowest balance card, the VISA. They'll keep going through this process, paying off cards in ascending order of their outstanding balance.

This strategy builds momentum. It's psychological. John and Tina will eliminate the Home Depot card quickly. They'll see and feel progress. Small victories will keep them motivated to continue and eventually pay off all their debt. With this strategy, John and Tina may pay more total interest, but they'll have a higher likelihood of success.

Pick the strategy that works for you. If you're highly disciplined, patient, and persistent, the Highest Interest Rate First strategy will work. If you need ongoing motivation, try the Lowest Balance first. Don't worry about finding the optimal solution. Don't start running creative calculations. Just pick an option, stick to it, and you'll pay off your credit card debt.

Once you're out of credit card debt, take the following steps:

- **Pay the balance in full:** Credit cards are great for convenience, protection, and building a credit history. If you pay your card in full each month, you get these benefits without the costs.

- **Pick your main card:** You only need one credit card. Your card should have online statements, fraud protection, rewards, and no annual fees. Notice I didn't say it should carry a low interest rate. It doesn't matter. If you pay your card in full each month, the interest rate is irrelevant. If you are unable or unwilling to do that, you shouldn't have a card.

- **Cut up other cards *(don't cancel them or close the accounts, unless they have annual fees)*:** 30% of your credit score is based on your credit utilization. This is the amount of credit you use divided by the amount of credit you have available. The lower the ratio, the better.

If you close or cancel cards, you lower the amount of credit available to you and increase your ratio. By cutting up cards, you ensure you don't use them while getting the benefit of having more available credit. I'm not suggesting you should open new cards simply to have more available credit. But, if you have them, simply cut them up.

- **Find alternatives:** If you can't control yourself, don't use credit cards. You have options. Cash, secured cards, and prepaid cards all work. Yes, they have their own drawbacks, but none have the downside of credit cards. Just ask someone in credit card debt.

- **Tell people about the dangers of credit cards:** Start telling people about the dangers of credit cards and you'll feel more pressure to be responsible with yours. You don't want to be a hypocrite, right?

There are tons of websites that provide information on credit cards. Most of these sites also make money by offering credit cards. Be careful. Use the sites for information. Don't get lured into getting a new card because you believe it will solve your problems. It won't.

For a good overview of your rights with credit cards and how to read your statements, look up the Credit Card Act of 2009 and check out federalreserve.gov/creditcard.

Private Student Loans

Student loans never die. Even in bankruptcy, you can't get rid of your student loans. It's important to pay them off.

There are two types of student loans: federal (owned by the government) and private (owned by a bank). It's hard to tell which types of loans you have by simply looking at them. To figure it out, you can call each lender or follow these steps:

1. Go to the National Student Loan Data System at nslds.ed.gov.

2. Click "Financial Aid Review."

3. Enter your information. If you don't remember your PIN or need to change it, click "Change PIN" and follow the directions. This will take a few days. Be patient.

4. Once you're in the database, it will show you all your federal loans and remaining balances.

5. All other student loans are private.

Your private student loans are top priority. Banks are less forgiving than the government. They know that you must pay back your student loans. They don't negotiate and rarely change payment terms. They're in a position of power which gives you few options. Government, on the other hand, offers deferment, forbearance, multiple payment options, and forgiveness programs. You can tackle these a little later.

Should I consolidate / refinance my loans?
It depends. First, let's understand what these terms mean.

- **Consolidation:** You give all your loans to one lender. Instead of owing multiple people, you will owe one. It's for convenience.

- **Refinancing:** You get a lower-interest rate loan to pay off your current loan. It can help you save on interest.

Notice that consolidating, refinancing, or doing anything else with your loans doesn't mean you're paying them off. All you're doing is changing the terms and whom you owe. Sure, you can save on interest in the long term, but you still need the discipline to build *fuel* and send out a check every month.

With that in mind, there are several refinancing/consolidation options to consider, one of which may be right for you, including:

- sofi.com.
- pave.com.
- upstart.com.
- commonbond.co.
- Your local credit union
- Your parents (in lucky cases)

Make sure there are low-to-no fees. Be careful of turning federal loans into private, because you'll lose any protections that came with your federal loans. And, if the process is stressful, just stop. Put your energy into building *fuel* each month and you'll get through it.

Medical Debt

Health insurance doesn't pay for all your medical costs. You're responsible for premiums, copays, coinsurance and deductibles. The challenge is knowing how much you truly owe. Hospitals and doctor's offices will collect from anywhere possible. If you're faced with medical bills and debt, take the following steps:

1. **Get organized:** Collect all your explanations of benefits (EOB) and medical billing statements in one place. They'll have details such as the date of service, procedure, etc. Some may not require payment, but you'll ultimately need to reconcile each of them and having everything in one place is helpful.

2. **Research:** Call your insurance company (or go online) and ask them:

   a. How your health plan works.

   b. For each bill, if the provider has submitted the claim to insurance.

   c. How much you owe on each and why. They will tell you if your portion is part of your deductible, coinsurance, copay, etc.

3. **Pay:** Once you've verified the bill, either pay or call the provider and ask for payment options. If you can't pay in full, they will set you up on a reasonable payment plan with little to no interest. If needed, you can try to negotiate the bill.

Medical practices rarely report delinquencies to credit agencies. But, they will send you to collections, which does impact your credit. It's easier to work out an arrangement with your medical provider than battle a collections company.

The health care system is complex and frustrating. The billing process is worse. Don't try to avoid it. It won't go away. Tackle it head-on and put a plan together. It's part of filling tank #3 and, as with other bad debt, will soon be part of your past.

Tax Debt

Tax debt creates stress, anxiety, and fear. The thought of wage garnishments, audits or even court can cause sleepless nights. Fortunately, for most people, attacking tax debt head-on will help avoid the wrath of Uncle Sam.

If you owe the US government money, always review your past tax returns to make sure you didn't miss any deductions or credits. In other words, confirm how much you owe and make sure it's correct. Then, you have two primary options:

- **Payment agreement:** A simple installment agreement will help you pay the debt with payments you can afford. The IRS generally provides low interest rates. They want to help you pay your taxes.

- **Offer in compromise:** You can ask the government to settle the debt for less. They will check on your ability to pay (remember, they have access to everything). If you can afford to make payments, they won't compromise. Very few offers are approved. If yours is approved, you will need to make payments quickly – they don't want to wait for the money if they have compromised. Also, offers to compromise don't hurt your credit (although getting approved probably means it's bad already).

Don't put off dealing with your tax debt. Start by calling the IRS. Understand your options. I know it sounds intimidating, but they can help. Often, you'll simply set up a payment plan and get it paid off over time.

Retirement Plan Loans

The good news is it's your money. That's why many consider a retirement plan loan from a 401(k), 403(b), or 457 plan as "not that bad". Wrong. They're dangerous. Here are a few reasons you should pay back your retirement plan loans as soon as possible:

- **60-day rule:** If you lose your job or leave your job, you must pay back retirement plan loans within 60 days. Otherwise, they will be considered a distribution, meaning you will owe taxes and a 10% penalty. That will hurt.

- **Lost earnings:** You've taken money out of your retirement account. It's no longer earning interest. You need to save and earn interest to reach your retirement goals. You've handicapped your own future.

- **Fees:** You often pay administration and maintenance fees to borrow your own money. You don't get these back.

- **Less monthly income:** You're required to start paying back your loans immediately. It's usually done through payroll deductions. In other words, your paychecks will be smaller. If you're already living check to check, this could cause problems and lead to more debt. Don't get caught in a vicious cycle.

- **No more protection:** The money in your retirement account is protected in bankruptcy. In other words, you get to keep it even if you need to declare bankruptcy. If you pull it out as a loan, it's no longer protected. That's no good.

- **Taxes:** Assume you borrow $10,000. Worst case scenario, you can't pay it back. In that case, it's considered a distribution. You will owe taxes and, if you're under 59 ½, a 10% penalty. If you're in the 25% tax bracket, you will own Uncle Sam $2,500 in taxes and $1,000 in penalties by April 15th. Can't pay that either? Now you have tax debt. It's a vicious cycle.

Borrowing from your retirement account can be enticing. No credit checks, it's a simple process, and it's your money. Don't be fooled. It's still debt, and it's still dangerous.

You should definitely avoid retirement loans to buy a home, pay for college, or pay off other debt. If you're in a jam, tap your emergency fund or home equity before your 401(k). If you already have a loan, pay it off in tank #3.

Not-So-Bad Debt

Keep making payments on these debts. You'll get a chance to pay them off as part in tank #7.

Federal Student Loans

You have options with your federal student loan debt. These options are constantly changing and have weird names. Go to nslds.ed.gov to get the details on your loans. You specifically need to understand how much of your federal student loans are direct loans (directly from the government) vs. FFELP loans (administered by a bank but follow federal loan rules). This distinction dictates your options.

Most people should simply make their monthly payments and pay off their student loans over time. If you can't make the payments, you have some choices.

- **Consolidation:** Consolidation puts all your loans into one payment. It makes life easier. The interest rate is the weighted average of your existing loans. It's lower than your highest rates and higher than your lowest rate. You don't always save money, but making one payment to one place is easier to manage.

- **Forbearance/deferment:** If you can't pay, you can request forbearance or deferment. Deferment defers your payments and stops interest from building on your subsidized loans. Forbearance simply stops payments but interest builds. Deferment is better than forbearance, but it's not your choice. You apply for both. The government will tell you what you qualify for.

- **Change payment schedule:** There are four types of payment options – standard, graduated, extended and income-based.

  o *Standard:* Everyone starts on the standard schedule. It's a 10-year repayment plan with the same payment each month.

  o *Graduated:* The graduated schedule also takes 10 years but has smaller payments in the beginning and larger payments towards the end.

  o *Extended:* The extended schedule only applies if you have over $30,000 in either FFELP or direct loans. It extends the number of years you pay, so your payment drops.

  o *Income-Based:* The income-based repayment (IBR) program sets your payment as a percentage of your discretionary spending. You need to apply with all your financials. Then, they give you a payment amount.

  Find the right payment schedule based on your situation. Go to studentaid.ed.gov for calculators that will show you your payments under the different schedules. Always remember that interest accrues. If you lower your payment, you will pay more in interest. There is no free lunch. It's math.

- **Loan forgiveness:** Wait, there is a free lunch. It's called loan forgiveness. But, as with the entire student loan world, it's confusing. There are different types of forgiveness programs.

o *Public Service Loan Forgiveness (PSLF):* If you take a qualified public service job, you only pay your student loans for 10 years. Select the extended or income-based repayment program to get the most benefit. After 10 years, all remaining federal student loans are forgiven. Don't worry, there is no impact to your credit and, in most cases, you're not taxed on the forgiven amount.

o *Professional-Based forgiveness:* Some professions (law, medical, military, Americorps, Peace Corps, businesses, etc.) have loan forgiveness incentives for working in public service. Some of these are through the PSLF while others have their own program. If you're considering public service or nonprofit jobs, check on your options for student loan forgiveness.

o *Income-based repayment (IBR):* If you're on an income-based repayment plan, your loans are forgiven after 25 years of payments. The government can be merciful. Except, with IBR, they tax you on anything they forgive. That hurts, but it's better than paying the full amount.

Overall, the government simply wants you to pay them back. They try to make it as painless as possible. Check out finaid.org and studentaid.ed.gov for great information on your options. Then, reach out to your loan servicer (the people that send you the statements) to figure out which option is right for you.

Auto Loans

It's okay to have a car payment. Yes, you read that correctly. It's okay to have a car payment. You need transportation. In cities like Atlanta, a car is mandatory. If it fits in your budget, and you can still have monthly *financial fuel*, make your payment and move on. If, on the other hand, you're drowning under your car payment, it's time for a change.

Here are a few ways to ease the pain of a car payment:

- **Change cars:** This is easier said than done, but it's not impossible. If you owe more than the car is worth, you're stuck. Keep making the payments until you owe less than it's worth.

  When you owe less than your car is worth, you've got options. Check kbb.com to determine the *'private party'* value of your car. List your car at the KBB 'private party' value on craigslist.com to gauge interest. The lowest you're willing to sell your car for is the amount you owe. Remember, you're simply trying to get out of the car payment and purchase something else that fits your budget.

- **Refinance:** Check with banks, credit unions and your current lender to see if you can refinance at a lower interest rate. Look for a lower interest rate with the same term. If you have 36 months left, refinance with a 36-month loan. Don't get drawn in by the 60-month loan just because that will drop your payment more. Stick with the same term and you'll win in the long run.

- **Share a ride:** Who do you know that could share in the payment? It's not common but, if you can find someone you trust who consistently needs a car, consider sharing. See if they will pay a portion of the note in return for using the car on specific days.

- **Rent your car:** It's now possible. Startups such as relayrides.com are making it easy to rent your car when you're not using it. Leave the renter a bottle of water and a nice note to get good reviews.

You may love your car. It's how you enjoy the journey and tolerate the 2-hour commute to work each day. There is nothing wrong with that. But, the numbers don't lie. If the payments are weighing down your plan, be honest with yourself. There will be another time to have some nice wheels.

Mortgage / Home Equity

You don't need to pay off your home early. It's an admirable goal, but it's not required to finish tank #3. Keep making on-time payments and you will pay off your home over time. The same holds true for home equity loans. If you have an outstanding loan, simply make the payments. Finish filling tanks #3, #4 and #5 before you consider adding payments to your mortgage or home equity. Then, we'll cover paying off your home early as part of your bucket list in tank #7.

Debt Pay off Strategies to <u>Avoid</u>

Consumer debt and credit is a multi-hundred billion dollar market. Companies make money by giving you credit and, on the flip side, getting you out of debt. There are endless advertisements on how some organization or company can get you out of debt quickly. They know most people are looking for a quick fix. They know you're vulnerable. Some can help but most hustle. Here are a few debt pay off strategies that are often too good to be true. They sound great but often leave you right back where you started or potentially in more debt.

Swapping debt

How about using one loan to pay off another? Don't get cute. Look your debt in the eye, set your plan, make life adjustments, and pay it off. It's a hard lesson. It's painful. But it will stick with you, and you won't go back into debt.

I needed to start out by saying that. I believe it. But, I understand there are unique situations where swapping debt could be beneficial. If you're in one of those situations, ask yourself the following:

- **How did you get into debt?:** If your behavior got you into debt, swapping for a lower interest rate won't get you out. You must address the underlying behavior. Credit card debt is one of many behavioral debts. You get out of it by using one of the strategies discussed in the credit card debt section.

- **Are you good with paying off debt?:** If you're always in debt, swapping debt won't help you. You're simply trading one problem for another. If you're good about paying off debt, swapping could save you money.

If you still believe you should swap debt after answering the questions above, make sure you fully understand the swap. Here are some common swaps and potential traps:

Use...	To pay off....	Rating	Watch out
Low- interest credit card	Higher- interest credit card	Average	You can save money but will likely stay in debt with the new card because you haven't addressed the behavioral issues.
Home equity	Private student loans	Average	If you have significant home equity, this could remove a debt that never goes away. If not, don't put your house on the line to save a few dollars.
Home equity	Credit cards	Average	If you have significant home equity, this could work. If not, don't put your house on the line to save a few dollars.
Any debt	Payday / Title loans	Average	You can save a lot if you don't go back to using these high- interest services.
Student loans	Credit cards	Bad	Student loans are much higher risk debt. They can't be discharged in bankruptcy. Don't do this.
Friend loan	Any	Average	You may destroy a relationship over money. Proceed cautiously.
401(k) loan	Private student loans	Bad	Money in your 401(k) is protected from creditors. If you take it out, it's no longer protected.

Notice that none of these debt swaps are considered "Good." They take your focus off the plan. They put a Band-Aid on a problem that needs surgery. And, you're still in debt after the swap.

Use your time and energy to increase your *financial fuel* and eliminate debt. You may pay a little more in the short term, but you will save days, months, and years of frustration.

Debt management and settlement

Every time I turn on the radio, I hear a commercial from a debt management or debt settlement company. They say,

"We can cut your payments in half."

"You may not owe your taxes."

"Stop the bill collectors from calling."

Unbelievable! If only it were that easy. If you're expecting another company to handle your debt problem, you're taking a risk. It's not free, you lose control, and often, you're still in debt after using the service. Consider the following:

- **High fees:** Settlement and management companies charge 15-20% of the outstanding balance for their services. If you owe $10,000, it will cost you $1,000 to get help.

- **Upfront fees:** They tell you to stop paying the creditor. You start paying them instead. Your first few payments go to them while your debt collects interest. If you miss later payments, you may be in a deeper hole than when you started. It's ugly.

- **Loss of control:** You got into debt. You hired them to get you out. Have you solved the problem or made it worse?

- **No recourse:** There are tons of scams in the debt settlement/management business. They might simply take your money and never pay a creditor. Sure, you can sue them, but with what money? It's the perfect industry for fraud.

- **Credit impact:** Settled debt shows up as "settled" on your credit report. It tells future lenders that you may only pay them back a portion of their money. Not good.

In dire situations (such as if you're near bankruptcy), contact a nonprofit like Clearpoint (credability.org) or Money Management International (www.mmi.org) to get help. Make sure you're involved in the process with monthly check-ins or manage your own debt. You can do it.

Bankruptcy

Bankruptcy is not a strategic choice. It's not even a choice. It's what you do when your financial life is broken and you've exhausted all other options. I often hear the word bankruptcy tossed around as if it's the same as deferring your student loans. It's not. It's painful and has consequences that go way beyond the credit report.

If you're thinking about bankruptcy, consider the following:

- **Trigger event:** Bankruptcy often happens after a major unexpected event such as extended unemployment, an illness, or divorce. It's not part of the natural flow of your financial life. If you don't have a distinct trigger event, ask yourself how you got into your financial situation. Bankruptcy may temporarily ease the pain, but it won't solve the problem.

- **Options:** Have you tried following the 7-Tank System? Have you visited a nonprofit credit counselor? Have you considered asking friends for help? Have you swallowed your pride? Have you done everything possible to avoid bankruptcy? Make sure you've exhausted all options before going this route.

- **Chapter 7 vs. Chapter 13:** There are two types of bankruptcy, Chapter 7 and Chapter 13. Chapter 7 says, "I can't pay at all," while Chapter 13 puts you on a payment plan. You don't get to choose. The default is Chapter 13. You must qualify to declare Chapter 7.

- **What you keep:** In Chapter 13, you're on a payment plan so you keep your house and car. In Chapter 7, you could lose everything, depending on the state. In both, you keep all money in your retirement accounts – your IRA, 401(k), 403(b), etc. This is another reason that you shouldn't take 401(k) loans!

- **You still may owe:** Bankruptcy does not get rid of all your debt. Child support, alimony, new tax debt, and student loans are still your responsibility. You're also on the hook for major purchases made within 90 days of the filing. Is it still worth it?

- **The future of your credit:** If you're considering bankruptcy, your credit should be the least of your concerns. It will take a hit for 7-10 years. Lenders will know about it even past that date. It may impact your ability to get a job. It will have other repercussions you can't predict. It's bad.

Do not take bankruptcy lightly. I never recommend bankruptcy, even when the math shows it's a good option. I tell clients to try everything else and then try those options again. If it happens to you, I hope this system will help you rebuild your life. But, if you can avoid the extremes of bankruptcy, even better.

> ### Note
> Before considering bankruptcy, let me again urge you to contact a nonprofit credit counseling agency such as Clearpoint (credability.org) or Money Management International (www.mmi.org) to get help. If you still can't get your finances in order, contact a trusted bankruptcy attorney. Don't go through the process alone.

Carter Family: #3 - Bad Debt Free

To complete tank #3, the Carter family needs to pay off bad debt. Here's a look at all of their debt:

Bad debt

Type of Debt	Date	Initial Amount	Interest Rate	Min Pmt	Current Balance
Private student loans	2011	$ 15,000	4.75%	$ 157	$ 9,717
Credit card	2015	$ 4,000	18.90%	$ 100	$ 4,000
Other high interest debt	2015	$ 1,500	99.00%	$ 200	$ 1,500
Total bad debt		**$ 20,500**		**$ 457**	**$ 15,217**

Not-so-bad debt

Type of Debt	Date	Initial Amount	Interest Rate	Min Pmt	Current Balance
Federal student loans	2011	$ 12,000	6.80%	$ 138	$ 8,054
Mortgage	2013	$ 250,000	4.50%	$ 1,650	$ 241,388
Car note	2013	$ 19,000	4.00%	$ 350	$ 11,541
Total not-so-bad debt		**$281,000**		**$2,138**	**$ 260,983**

They can keep making payments on the not-so-bad debt (mortgage, car, and federal student loans). It's time to pay off the rest. The total current balance on bad debt is ~$15,200. Feels like a ton, but they can do it. They decide they will use the 'Highest Interest First' strategy.

They have $150 of *financial fuel*. As they pay off each debt, they will no longer have those payments. As a result, their *fuel* will increase and they can make bigger payments on the next debt. For example, when they pay off the $1,500 of "other high interest debt", they no longer need to make that payment and can add that *fuel* to the credit cards. It's called debt laddering and is a powerful tool for paying off debt.

By using debt laddering, it will take the Carters ~33 months to pay off their bad debt[4]. That's a little over 2.5 years. Two and half years will be gone before they know it – might as well be debt free.

[4] We used the Carter family's debt amortization schedules and debt laddering to calculate 33 months.

#4 - Emergency Fund to Cover 3-6 Months

Freedom is close. You can taste it. You've paid off all your bad debt. It's a huge accomplishment. Don't downplay it. Tell the world. Celebrate. Party like a rock star. Just stay within the budget.

Now, it's time to build your emergency fund to cover 3-6 months of core expenses. The specific amount recommended for you is based on your risk factors. For example, if you have low job security or a high chance of illness, you should have closer to six months put away. If you have high job security and a low chance of illness, three months may be fine. Be conservative. More savings are always better than less. And, since you no longer have bad debt payments, you should have more monthly *financial fuel* to build your fund!

Here are a few additional details on tank #4.

Where do I invest it?

Put a month's worth of expenses in your checking or savings account (where it can be immediately accessible). Put the remaining in very low-risk investments such as money market accounts or bank certificates of deposit (CDs).

When do I use it?

When you have an emergency. You will get a flat tire. Your roof will spring a leak. You may lose your job. Your spouse may get ill so you need to take time off. Life happens. It's unpredictable. A full emergency fund removes at least some of the resulting financial stress.

What do I do after I use it?

Replenish it. If you use $500 from your fund, put it back before moving on with your plan. You will refill your emergency fund multiple times in the early part of your journey. Eventually, you'll have enough saved beyond the emergency fund so that you'll never touch it.

◎ Carter Family: #4 - Emergency Fund to Cover 3-6 Months

The Carter family wants to build a 4-month emergency fund of $12,000. They will save enough for one month ($3,000) when they fill tank #2. So, to fill tank #4, they will need an additional three months of saving ($9,000).

When they get to this tank, the Carter family will no longer have $460/month of bad debt payments. They can add that amount to their original $150 of *financial fuel*. Therefore, their *fuel* to fill tank #4 will be $610/month. That's fantastic! With that *fuel*, it will take them ~15 months ($9,000/$610 = ~15) to build their 4-month fund.

They will invest their emergency fund as follows:

- $3,000 (1-month of core expenses) sits in their savings account at his bank. They can write checks against this account if there's an emergency.

- $9,000 (the remaining emergency fund) is put in a 6- or 12-month CD. It will earn 1% interest. Not great, but very safe. As interest rates increase, they can renew at the higher rate. If they need to withdraw early, the penalty is usually the accrued interest. That's okay. They're using the money for an emergency. A CD gives them the upside of some interest, with no downside of losing the $9,000 in principal.

Let's recap. In 64 months (~five years), the Carter family will have no bad debt and $12,000 cash in the bank. It will be an amazing feeling. They know five years will pass no matter what they do. They're not taking shortcuts. Their path is clear. They're following the 7-Tank System. Their son will be watching and learning how to be smart with money. It's a powerful journey that will impact their family for generations.

Note

Your 3-6 month emergency fund is not savings for a down payment on a new home. I know it's difficult to look at thousands of dollars in an account and not feel like you can use it. You can't. It's your safety net. It gives you true freedom. It buys you time and options. Don't cut holes in your safety net.

#5 - 20% of Gross Income to Retirement

Never run out of money. Never be dependent on your kids. That's how you build wealth that gets passed down for generations. That's true love. It's the best gift you can ever give your family. Welcome to tank #5. Filling this tank sets you free and lets you leave a little something when you go.

To fill tank #5, put 20% of your gross income into retirement every month. Yes, the number is 20%. It includes any match you get from your employer. If your employer gives you 5%, you need to contribute 15%. If they give you 2%, you need 18%. If there is no match, you're on your own for the entire 20%.

Before thinking about Roth vs. traditional, 401(k) vs. IRA or specific investments, make sure you are on a path to putting 20% of your gross income into retirement. With no debt payments and a full emergency fund, this should be easier. If necessary, build up to it. The goal is to get to 20%.

So why do I recommend 20%? I've taken the following retirement planning steps for hundreds of families and got the same result:

- **Retirement 1: Know your sources of income for retirement** (and how much you will get).
  Understand all the different ways you can make money during retirement.

- **Retirement 2: Calculate how much you need**.
  Calculate *"Your Retirement Number."* This is the amount you need to maintain your lifestyle and never run out of money.

- **Retirement 3: Calculate how much you must save each month to reach *"Your Retirement Number"*.**
  Break down your retirement number into the amount you should put away each month to get there.

- **Retirement 4: Decide where to save it.**
  Select retirement accounts (employer vs. IRA, Roth vs. traditional, etc.) and specific investments.

Let's take a look at each step.

Retirement 1: Know your sources of income for retirement.

Working, pension, Social Security, and your savings/investments. That's it. Those are all the ways you can make money during retirement. Only one is completely in your control, your savings. The others are full of uncertainty.

Working

You love your job. You plan to work forever. I completely understand. I feel the same way. Unfortunately, less than 20% of people work after retirement and, for many of them, it's out of their control. Illness, disability, downsizing, and being replaced by younger employees is part of reality. Be prepared. Don't assume you will be able to work until you die.

Pension

Pensions are vanishing. According to the Employee Benefits Research Institute, only 20% of employers offer pensions today. If you're a teacher, police officer, or firefighter, you may have a pension. If so, call your pension administrator and ask them:

- **How much is your pension expected to pay every month when you retire?** If it's a lump sum, ask the expected amount. If it's monthly, make sure you get a monthly amount adjusted for inflation.

- **What do you need to do to get that pension?** There are lots of rules including when you can retire and how many years of service you need. Every situation is unique.

If you don't have a pension, move on.

Social Security

Social Security is the most certain of the uncertain. It sounds crazy. The national debt is in the trillions. The baby boomer population is nearing retirement. Our government can't spend less than it makes (maybe they should read this book). Still, you must account for Social Security when planning for retirement. Otherwise, the amount you need to save is beyond comical.

First, you'll need to get your expected benefits from the Social Security Administration by setting up an account at ssa.gov/myaccount/. Then, you should understand the nuances of your Social Security benefit.

Let's take a look at John and Tina Carter's Social Security.

◎ The Carter Family Social Security

John and Tina looked up their Social Security benefit and found the following:

When it's taken	John	Tina
At full retirement age (67)	$1,934 a month	$1,407 a month
At age 70	$2,412 a month	$1,751 a month
At early retirement age (62)	$1,340 a month	$975 a month

For tank #5, John and Tina will focus on their estimated benefit at full retirement age (highlighted). It shows how much they will get each month <u>for life</u> when they retire. A few important nuances:

- **It's an estimate:** The payout figures assume John and Tina will continue to make the same amount of money (or more) until retirement. Social Security payouts are based on how much you contribute as part of your taxes. If they make more, they will have a higher payout. If they makes less, they can expect a lower payout.

- **Age matters (a lot):** John will get $1,934/month if he retires at a normal retirement age of 67. If he wants to retire early at 62, he will only get $1,340/month. If he waits until 70, he'll get $2,412/month. Tina will get $975/month at 62, $1,407/month at 67, and $1,751 at 70. The longer they can wait, the better.

- **It's inflation-adjusted:** Prices go up over time. So does your Social Security payout. The payouts increase ~3% per year to account for inflation. John is 34 years old. His $1,934/month payout today will be ~$6,000/month when he's 67. It feels like a big number but remember that all prices increase over time. In

30 years, a gallon of milk will be $8.50 and gas may cost $8/gallon.

- **There's a ceiling:** No matter how much John makes, his maximum Social Security benefit at 67 will be ~$2,650/month[5]. The same holds true for Tina. The more they make, the more they will be dependent on their own savings to maintain their lifestyle.

- **It can be taxed:** Up to 85% of social security payouts can be taxed. The more you make during retirement, the more likely your payout will be taxed.

- **It's reduced if you earn:** If John or Tina work during retirement, their payout could be reduced. In 2014, Social Security payouts were reduced $1 for every $3 of earnings over $42,000. These numbers will change, but the point will remain the same. You can't fully double dip by working and collecting Social Security.

For now, all the Carter family needs to know is that John will get $1,934/month and Tina will get $1,407/month when each retires (adjusted for inflation). The rest is on them.

Your Savings

This is your lifeline. The more you save, the better. You can't predict if you will work, pensions are limited, and while you will get Social Security, who knows how much? All you can control is how much you save this month, next month, next year, and for each year until you retire. Save enough and enjoy

[5] $2,663 is the maximum Social Security payout for 2015. This maximum payout adjusts for inflation each year.

Florida's white sand beaches. Fall short, and you may be sharing a bunk bed with the grandchildren.

The next few sections will show you how much you need to save and how to get there.

Retirement 2: Calculate how much you'll need.

So how much do you need to save in total? It's called *"Your Retirement Number."* It's the amount you'll need to maintain your lifestyle during retirement. Knowing your number helps you plan. It's not exact. When you see it, you may fall out of your chair. Don't stress. It will take time and it will help you understand why you need to save 20% of your gross income each month.

Let's calculate the Carter family's retirement number:

- John is 34 years old, Tina is 32 years old.
- $90,000/year combined household gross income.
- $40,000/year expected from Social Security (see retirement step 1).
- $14,000 in retirement savings from old jobs.

Exhibit 8 shows you how we calculated John and Tina's retirement number. Read the footnotes for details on each step. Then, calculate *"Your Retirement Number"* by entering your data into the chart. It will be big. Don't get discouraged.

John and Tina will need to save $1,931,875 by the time they retire at 67. They have $14,000. There's a long way to go but they can get there.

Exhibit 7: Calculating the Carter family's retirement number

Step	Amount
Enter current gross annual income	$90,000
x % of income you will need in retirement [1]	x 75%
= How much you need each year in retirement	= $67,500
- expected annual social security [2]	- $40,000
- expected annual pensions	- $0
= How much your savings needs to provide each year	= $27,500
x by 25 [3]	x 25
= Amount you need to save before retirement	= $687,500
x by inflation factor (see table)	x 2.81
Your Number[4]	$1,931,875

[1] On average, during retirement, people spend 70-80% of what they did before retirement.

[2] Multiply your expected monthly social security by 12. You can find this number on your online statement.

[3] Multiplying by 25 is the 4% Rule. The 4% rules states that if you only withdraw 4% from your savings each year, you will not outlive your money. That's good.

[4] This is how much you need when you retire. Take a deep breath.

Inflation factor table (to use in calculation above)

Years to Retirement	Inflation Factor
10	1.34
15	1.56
20	1.81
25	2.09
30	2.43
35	2.81
40	3.26
45	3.78

Retirement 3: Calculate how much you need to save each month to reach "Your Retirement Number".

Your number will be big. Look at it again. Okay, it's really big. Don't worry, you have time. But, you need to figure out how much you must save each month to get there. Let's continue with John and Tina Carter.

◎ John and Tina are in their early thirties and have $14,000 saved for retirement. So, how much do they need to save each month going forward to reach their number?

They go to bankrate.com and use their savings calculator. Currently, that calculator is located at the following site: www.bankrate.com/calculators/savings/saving-goals-calculator.aspx. They plug in the following numbers into the Bankrate calculator.

Question on bankrate calculator	Answer
How much do you want to save?	$1,931,875
How many years do you have in which to save it?	34 [1]
What interest rate do you expect to earn on your savings?	5%
Compounding	Monthly
How much money can you spare for your first deposit?	$14,000 [2]
Do you wish to skip savings 2 weeks each year?	No
Date of first deposit	Current date
Amount they need to save monthly	**$1,735**

[1] *Retirement at 67 minus their average age 33.*

[2] *Use the amount you already have in retirment savings.*

The calculator shows John and Tina will need to put away ~$1,735 each month to reach their number. It's 23% of their gross income. It's a little higher than 20% because they haven't saved enough and need to catch up. Still, it's possible. Here's how:

Source	Amount
John's current retirement contribution	$230 *(see tank #1)*
John's employer match	+ $115 *(see tank #1)*
Pretax *financial fuel* after filling tank #4	+ $800 [1]
Additional monthly savings	+ $590 (see below)
Total	**= $1,735**

[1] *This is their $610 of financial fuel before taxes.*

John and Tina will save $1,145/month for retirement through their current retirement contributions ($230), employer match ($115) and *financial fuel* after filling tank #4 ($800). Therefore, they will need to save an additional $590/month to reach their goal of $1,735 per month. It's not impossible. It won't happen overnight. But, with a few salary increases, a little hustle on getting extra income and a few expense cuts, they can do it.

When you calculate 'your retirement number', it may feel crazy. Don't get discouraged. There are thousands of people who live on 20% less than you and do just fine. You got this. You're debt-free and have 3-6 months of cash in the bank. With fewer payments, putting 20% away for retirement is very possible. Adjust your lifestyle, work overtime, find other ways to make money, and cut where you can. You're in control.

Retirement 4: Decide where to save it.

You've committed to saving 20% of your gross income. You know it will take time to get there, but you're on the path. The next question is where to put it.

This is a two-step process.

1. First, you need to decide on the <u>type</u> of account.
2. Second, you need to <u>select investments</u> within those accounts.

Most people do this at the same time, but it's easier to understand as two steps. Let's look at each.

1. Which <u>types</u> of accounts should you use for retirement?

There are two major decisions you need to make with selecting the right retirement account - Roth vs. traditional and employer retirement plans vs. individual retirement accounts (IRAs). Let's review these one at a time.

Roth vs. Traditional

Roth retirement accounts use after-tax money. There is no tax benefit today. In return, you don't pay taxes when you withdraw the funds at retirement. This is fantastic. It means that all the money in your Roth account is yours. You've already paid taxes and can plan accordingly.

Traditional retirement accounts use pre-tax money. You don't pay taxes on your contributions today. Your take home pay will be a little higher. That sounds good, but remember you will pay taxes when you withdraw. It's tough to plan accordingly.

Go with Roth if you're...

- Young.
- In a lower tax bracket.

- Don't think you'll need all the money you've saved and want to pass some of it down to future generations (wouldn't that be nice?)
- In doubt.

Employer Retirement Plan vs. Individual Retirement Account

First, let's define these.

- **Employer Retirement Plan:** 401(k), 403(b), 457, Roth 401(k), Roth 403(b), Roth 457, and any other retirement account with a similarly boring name.

- **Individual Retirement Account:** IRAs or Roth IRAs.

If you have a matching plan (tank #1), you'll need to use your employer retirement plan to get that match. Do that first. After you've reached the match amount, choosing between an IRA or adding more to your employer plan is a tough call. Most people simply add more to their employer plan. It's easy. Others switch to an IRA to save on fees or take advantage of the Roth option.

Let's take a look at a few factors that you should consider when deciding between your employer's plan and an IRA (after the match):

- **Fees:** This is the biggest factor. Employer plans are notorious for having high fees. And, until recently, they were hidden. On the exact same investment, you could pay ¼ percent to ½ percent more in your 401(k) vs. in an IRA. That's huge. It sounds small but, over time, it's big. Here's a comparison of two funds that have very similar investments and are expected to have the same performance but have different fees:

Name	Fees	10-years	20-years	30-years
Fund 1 (higher fees)	1.15%	$ 46,963	$ 121,880	$ 241,391
Fund 2 (lower fees)	0.65%	$ 48,383	$ 129,560	$ 265,758
Difference		$ 1,420	$ 7,680	$ 24,367

Wow! The fund with lower fees will save you $24,367 over 30 years. It's only ½ percent lower in fees but that makes a big difference over time. Try to pay less than .75 percent in fees for retirement investments. The lower, the better.

o   Advantage – **IRA**

- **Roth Option:** Does your employer offer a Roth 401(k)? If not, you'll need to go with an IRA to take advantage of the Roth option. Once you've contributed the maximum in your Roth IRA, you can go back to your employer plan.

    o   Advantage – **IRA** (if your employer does not offer a Roth option)

- **Convenience:** Your employer plan is usually a few clicks away. It pulls money from your paycheck. You don't need to think about it. And, they are easy to change, adjust, and monitor. IRAs, on the other hand, need to be set up. It's not hard, but it takes time. You'll need to research different options including traditional investment firms such as Vanguard and Fidelity and newer models such as Betterment.com and Wealth-Front.com. Once again, it's not hard, but will you take the time to do it right? If not, use the employer plan.

    o   Advantage – **Employer retirement plans**

- **Investment Options:** IRAs have more investment options. Your employer plan should have enough options to find what you need. Don't overcomplicate this. More options is not necessarily better. In fact, it can be more confusing.

  o Advantage – **Tied**

Remember, if you have a match, contribute to the employer plan first. Then, in tank #5, you can decide on your employer's plan vs. an IRA. Don't over-analyze. Get started with whichever option is easiest. When you have time, make adjustments.

2. Which investments should you choose?

After deciding on the right type of retirement account, you'll need to select investments. Remember, retirement investing is for the long run. It's to protect you from running out of money. It's not to get rich. There are hundreds of books and articles that dive deep into investing. This isn't one of them. Here's the short answer on how to invest your retirement savings:

- **Buy mutual funds:** All your retirement investments should be in mutual funds. Don't buy individual stocks. Funds make sure you don't have all your eggs in one basket. They help you diversify. They're smart.

- **Use passive funds:** Mutual funds come in two broad flavors - passive and active. Sadly, funds don't tell you which flavor they are. Instead, you figure it out by the name and fees.

  o *Passive funds* include index funds and target date funds. They buy the same stocks that are in an index. For example, the "Vanguard 500 Index Fund" buys the same stocks as the S&P 500. They don't think or analyze. They're simply saying, "We will copy the S&P 500." They're also cheap. Since they follow an index, there's not a lot of work for a manager and therefore, the fees are low.

o *Active funds*, on the other hand, have their own strategy. They say, "We can beat the index if we make our own choices." They have smart fund managers that pick stocks and try to beat the index. You pay higher fees for these funds. But, they rarely beat index funds. Go figure.

Use passive funds in your retirement account.

- **Get safer as you get older:** Safe investments include bonds, treasuries, money market funds, and cash. Risky investments include stock-based mutual funds.

o *The rule of thumb* is your age should equal the percentage of your money you have in safe investments. If you're 30, put 30% of your money into safe investments and 70% into more risky investments. If you're 60, 60% of your money should be in safe investments. Why? Because, when you're younger, you can take more risks and have enough time to weather the ups and downs of the economy. As you get older, and closer to needing the money, you want to take fewer risks. Don't gamble. Many near-retirees took major risks from 2005-2007 because the market was booming. They paid for it in 2008 when the market tanked.

- o *Target date funds* (a type of passive fund) are a simple way to mix safe and risky investments. They usually have names such as Target Date or Lifecycle with a date on the end. That date is the year you expect to retire. For example, Vanguard Target Retirement 2050 is designed for someone who will retire around 2050. That means they are probably 30 years old today. These funds change their mix of safe stuff and risky investments each year — getting safer as you get older. They're usually more risky than the rule of thumb, but they still do a good job.

Rules and Restrictions

Once you've decided on the type of account and investments, it's important to understand the rules and restrictions for your retirement savings.

Retirement accounts are tax-deferred – which means you don't get taxed on your gains while your money is growing in one of these accounts. Tax-deferred accounts save you money. It's Uncle Sam's way of encouraging you to save. That's good. In exchange, there are a few rules you must follow.

- • **Income Limits:** You're generally eligible for your employer's retirement plan regardless of how much you make. IRAs, on the other hand, have income limits. If you make too much, you can't contribute and get the tax benefit. There are different income limits for traditional IRAs and Roth IRAs based on your filing status. Check out irs.gov to find this year's limits. Remember, they change each year.

- **Contribution Limits:** In 2015, you can contribute a maximum of $5,500 to an IRA and $18,000 to your employer's retirement plan. These limits are per person. These limits go up if you're over 50. If you want to save more, you can, but just not in a retirement account.

- **No Withdrawal:** You can't take your money out until you are 59 ½. If you do, you will get hit with taxes and a 10% penalty. There are some exceptions, but who cares? Don't withdraw retirement savings for expenses today. Your retirement savings are for retirement. Even if special circumstances allow you to withdraw, don't do it. Find another way.

Rules and restrictions for retirement accounts adjust each year. Stay current once a year on the latest rules.

Don't overcomplicate retirement investing.

1) Focus on getting to 20% of gross income going to retirement.

2) Make sure you're using either your employer retirement plan (401(k), 403(b), etc.) or an individual retirement accounts (IRA).

3) Invest in a mix of safer and riskier funds based on how long you have until retirement.

Remember, retirement investing is not to get rich. Instead, your goal is to make sure you don't run out of money.

So, now what do you do? Actions speak louder than words. Let's summarize the Carter family's path for filling tank #5.

⦿ Carter Family: #5 - 20% of Gross Income to Retirement

When they arrive at tank #5, the Carters will have $12,000 in the bank and no debt. They will be feeling great. Then, it will be time to push the accelerator on retirement. Let's recap their retirement steps:

- **Retirement 1: Know your sources of retirement income**.
  The Carters don't have pensions. They don't want to work during retirement. They checked their recent Social Security statements and found they are eligible for the following at age 67:

    o   John Carter - $1,934/month
    o   Tina Carter - $1,407/month

- **Retirement 2: Calculate how much you need.**
  The next step was calculating their number. John and Tina will need to save $1,931,875 by the time they retire at 67. They have $14,000. After seeing that number, they probably need a glass of wine.

- **Retirement 3: Calculate how much you need to save each month to reach "Your Retirement Number".**
  John and Tina used the bankrate.com savings calculator to figure out how much they need to save each month to reach their number. The calculation shows they will need to save $1,735/month to reach their retirement goal. It's 23% of their gross income. It feels impossible but it's not. When they get to tank #5, they

will be debt free and have a full emergency fund. They both understand it won't happen overnight but they will get there.

- **Retirement 4: Decide where you save it.**
  This is where it gets fun. Over time, John and Tina will be socking away $1,735/month for retirement. They're working with real money. Choosing which types of accounts and investments should be less stressful. Here's what they've decided to do for tank #5:

Select type(s) of account:

  - After filling tank #4, John will increase his 401(k) contribution from 5% (tank #1) to 17.5%. Remember, he only needs to get to 17.5% because his employer will match 50% of the first 5% (or 2.5%). He makes $4,583/month pre-tax. His 17.5% contribution will put $800/month to retirement plus $115/month for the match.

    John will not use an IRA because the 401(k) is convenient and he is comfortable with their online site.

  - Tina will open an IRA and contribute $450/month. She doesn't want to use her 401(k) because the fees were significantly higher. At that amount, she will reach her $5,500/year contribution limit. If she wants to contribute more, she can use her employer's 401(k).

- o Together, John and Tina will be putting in $1,365/month towards retirement. It's not $1,735 yet, but they'll get there. They're determined to be wealthy and on the right path.

Select investments:

- o John and Tina will both use target date funds.

- o John's 401(k) offers Vanguard funds. John is eyeing the Vanguard Retirement 2045 Fund since he will be ~67 in 2045. The total expense ratio on that fund is ~.5%, which is great.

- o Tina is considering an IRA with Fidelity. Fidelity's target date funds are called Freedom Funds. Tina likes the Fidelity Freedom Fund 2050 since she will be 67 by ~2050. The expense ratio on this fund is 0.77%. Not great but okay.

- o Each year, John and Tina will check their funds as part of their investment review. They may make changes, but target date funds are a great place to start for retirement.

For tank #5, the Carters are on their way to putting 20% of the gross income towards their retirement. That's awesome. They will love themselves for making this choice. It's a little painful calculating and making sense of the numbers. But, they trust the system and are on the smart path.

#6 - Children's College

If you have *financial fuel* <u>after</u> putting 20% towards retirement, save for your children's college. The key word in the previous sentence is <u>after</u>. Read the note at the end of this section to understand why the order matters. Retirement first, then college.

Okay, you get it. You're saving for retirement and have more money for college. Impressive. Take these steps to make figure out how much to save for your children's college:

- **College 1: Figure out how much you will need.**
  College tuition is rising 6% per year. You'll need a lot to pay it.

- **College 2: Understand all the different ways to pay for college.**
  This should be a combination of your money, loans, and your kid's money. It's a team effort.

- **College 3: Decide which type(s) of account(s) to use.**
  Use Coverdell and 529s to take advantage of the tax benefits.

- **College 4: Select your investments.**
  Investments should go from aggressive to more conservative as kids get closer to attending college.

Let's walk through each step.

College 1: Figure out how much you will need.

On average, college costs have increased 6% per year for the past 50 years. That's twice the rate of increase for milk, bread, stamps, healthcare costs and, for most people, income. It's insane. At this rate, the average annual college tuition in 2030 will be $39,700 for public schools and $95,800 for private schools. Yes, that's nearly one hundred grand for one year of college.

If costs keep growing at this rate, here's the estimated tuitions you can expect in the near future:

	2015	2020	2025	2030	2035
Public	$ 16,900	$ 22,500	$ 29,900	$ 39,700	$ 52,900
Private	$ 38,900	$ 52,600	$ 71,000	$ 95,800	$ 129,400

Are you kidding me? I've looked these numbers over a thousand times and they still give me acid reflux. When I first calculated them, they didn't make sense. What is $95,800 in 2030? How could I ever save over $400,000? No chance. Put up the white flag. I give up.

Okay, back to reality. Let's make these crazy numbers easier to understand with the following question - *How much do you need to save each month to have enough to pay for college?*

This question puts college costs into perspective.

Let's look at the Carter family as an example:

- John is 34 years old, Tina is 32 years old.
- Atlanta residents.
- 2-year-old son, Willy.
- Great local public schools: Georgia Tech, University of Georgia, and Georgia State.

- Want to keep private schools as an option just in case Willy throws a tantrum at eighteen about where he wants to go.

John and Tina use the chart and table below to calculate how much they need to save each month to pay for Willy's college:

Description	Carter family
Current cost of 1 year of college	$ 22,250
x Cost factor	x 2.54
Estimated future cost of 1 year of college	$ 56,515
x Years in college	x 4.00
Estimated total cost of college	$ 226,060
x Savings factor	x .0034
Required monthly savings	$ 769

Cost and savings factor table

Years Until College	Cost Factor	Savings Factor
1	1.06	0.0814
2	1.12	0.0397
3	1.19	0.0258
4	1.26	0.0189
5	1.34	0.0147
6	1.42	0.0199
7	1.50	0.01
8	1.59	0.0085
9	1.69	0.0074
10	1.79	0.0064
11	1.90	0.0057
12	2.01	0.0051
13	2.13	0.0046
14	2.26	0.0041
15	2.40	0.0037
16	2.54	0.0034
17	2.69	0.0031
18	2.85	0.0029

Don't get overwhelmed. There are lots of numbers on that page. Just enter your numbers into the same table as John and Tina as follows:

- **Current cost of 1 year of college:** Pick a school nearby that your child could attend. Look up the total cost for a year on their website. Enter the number. Don't worry, this is just giving you an estimate.

  o The Carter family selected Georgia Tech, with in-state costs of $22,250/y ear

- **Cost and savings factors:** Look at the table. Find the number of years until your kid goes to college (from 1-20). Enter the cost and savings factors in the right places of the equation. Then, do the math.

  o Willy is 2 years old and has 16 years until college. The cost factor for 16 years is 2.54. The savings factor for 16 years is .0034.

The Carter family needs to save $769/month for the next 16 years to pay for Willy's college. That may be realistic. It may feel impossible. Fortunately, your savings is not the only source of funds for your kid's college. It's not all on you. Move to the next section.

College 2: Understand the different ways to pay for college

There are tons of options to pay for college. Grants, scholarships, work-study, Stafford loans, PLUS loans, 529s, Coverdell, the list goes on. It's not all on you.

Here's the big picture. These are all the ways you, or your child, can get money for college.

How your child can pay	How you (parent) can pay
• **Free money**	• **Savings plans**
o Pell Grant	o 529 plans
o FSEOG	o Coverdell plans
o Armed Forces	o Series EE bonds
o Scholarships	• **Borrowed money**
• **Borrowed money**	o PLUS loans
o Stafford loans	o Bank loans
o Perkins loans	
o Bank loans	
• **Their money**	
o Work-study	
o Off-campus jobs	
o Savings	

Let's look at each.

How the student (your child) can pay

It's their college. It's their future. Sure, you love them and want to help, but they must be part of the process. There are multiple ways your child can get money for college.

- **Free money:** This is money you don't pay back.

  - *Pell Grants:* This is the largest grant program for undergrads based on financial need. You don't need to apply. After completing the FAFSA (Free Application for Federal Student Aid), they will tell you if your child qualifies and how much they get.

- ○ *FSEOG (Federal Student Education Opportunity Grant):* This is another federal grant based on need. Like the Pell Grant, you complete the FAFSA and they decide if your child qualifies and how much they get.

- ○ *Armed forces:* By joining the armed forces, your child can serve the country, build character, learn team skills and get money for college. It's not for everyone, but can help.

- ○ *Scholarships:* There are thousands of scholarships. Every one of them is different. Most have their own applications. Some are very specific. Your child should apply for as many as possible. It takes work. It will take time on the weekend. Your child needs to do this work for their own future. Here are few ways to start your search:

  - ▪ *School career center:* Your child's high school counselor, graduation coach, or favorite teacher is a great place to start. They generally have a database of scholarships that past students have won. Reach out to those students to get further guidance.

  - ▪ *Local service organizations:* With scholarships, it's all local. Organizations such as Kiwanis, Rotary, and others have scholarship programs. Reach out directly to understand their requirements and deadlines.

  - ▪ *Friends'/Family's companies:* Most major companies have scholarship programs. Ask friends and family to check at their company and then apply.

- *Scholarship search engines:* Most people report mediocre results, but it's a worth a shot to understand who's offering money. Some good sites include chegg.com, cappex.com and scholarships.com. Don't ever pay for these sites! Remember, these sites make money through advertising. Use an email address dedicated to scholarship search to avoid being spammed.

Yes, there are a lot of these. It takes work. Your child should write essays from the heart. Apply to every single one — there is nothing to lose.

- **Borrowed money:** These are loans. Your child will have debt. At the same time, it makes them more responsible for their education. They will value it more. And, you can continue to support them as needed.

  - *Stafford loans:* These are federal loans. They usually have set rates and terms. They can be subsidized (the loan doesn't accrue interest until your child graduates) or unsubsidized (the loan accrues interest from the moment your child takes out the loan). Most students have Stafford loans. They're not bad.

  - *Perkins loans:* These are low-interest federal loans based on need. These are great if your child qualifies. The school will tell you.

- o *Bank loans:* These loans, also known as private student loans, are between your child and the bank. They generally have variable interest rates. They have very few protections. Be careful.

- **Their money:** Your kid can work. Here are ways they can earn money.

  - o *Work-study:* This is part of your child's financial aid package. Jobs are generally on campus. Working while in school requires discipline and time management. It's no different than playing a sport. It's not impossible.

  - o *Off-campus job:* If there are no work-study options, your child can find a job. Once again, working while in school requires discipline and time management. They can do it.

  - o *Savings:* Your child can earn before going to college. Summer jobs, chores, etc. They can make money. Let them. Also let them use their money to pay for their education.

How you (parent) can pay

I understand. Whether you still hate paying your own student loans or your parents paid for your college, you want to help your child pay for school. Here are some of your options:

- **Savings plans:** Just like retirement, saving for college also has tax-deferred accounts. They're similar to an IRA or 401(k), except they're for college.

- *529s:* These are the largest type of tax-deferred college savings plans. You put money in, pick an investment, watch it grow, and use the proceeds for college. There are over 100 different 529 plans. It's confusing. We'll review them in the next section.

- *Coverdell Education Savings Account (ESA):* The Coverdell ESA is similar to the 529 plan but it has a $2,000 limit and a few different rules. Most brokerage firms and banks offer Coverdell ESAs. They have different fees and investment options. Shop around. We'll also look at these in the next section.

- *Series EE bonds:* These are government bonds with no taxes on the interest. That's good. They also generally have low returns. That's not good when college costs are skyrocketing.

- **Borrowed money:** Parents can also take loans. This is not ideal but it's possible. Remember, student loans can't be discharged in bankruptcy. Be careful. Here are the options:

  - *Plus loans:* These are federal loans. They allow parents with good credit to borrow for education.

  - *Bank loans:* These are standard loans from a bank. Take them out at your own risk.

That's it. Notice, I did not include pulling from your 401(k) or IRA. Tank #5 comes before tank #6. Don't pull from your future — it hurts everyone.

College 3: Decide on the type(s) of accounts

You understand all the ways your child can pay for college. Still, you want to help by saving a little for them. That's the point of adding *fuel* to tank #6.

There are two smart ways to save for education, 529 plans and Coverdell plans. Both plans allow your money to grow tax-free if you use the funds for qualified education expenses (tuition, books, board, etc.). That means that if you make $2,000 or $200,000 in interest in a college savings account, you don't pay taxes on those gains. That's huge!

Now, let's get into the details on which plan to choose, the steps to make it happen, and some of the rules.

529 vs. Coverdell

Here are some key differences between 529 plans and Coverdell plans:

	529	Coverdell
To qualify, you can make up to...	Whatever (no limit)	$110,000 (single), $220,000 (married)
You can contribute up to...	Very High	$2,000/year
You can use the money for...	College	Private elementary, middle, high, and college
You must use the money...	Any age	By 30 years old
You can transfer to....	Eligible family member	Eligible family member under 30
You can deduct your contributions from...	State taxes (varies by state and plan)	None

Notice a few important differences:

- There are no income limits on 529s. Anyone can use them.

- Coverdell plans only allow $2,000/year per child. That's a total for everyone contributing. You can't have the grandparents open a separate account and exceed the limit.

- Coverdell funds can be used for any school including private K-12 education.

- You can get a state tax deduction for 529s if you get your state's plan and they offer the deduction.

So which one is better? It depends. I hate that answer. In most situations, contribute $2,000 to the Coverdell first, then open a 529. Good K-12 education prepares your child for college. No point in saving for college if they're not ready when they go. If you don't use the Coverdell funds for K-12, you can use it for college. Flexibility is good.

Selecting a plan
Coverdell plans are easy. You can open one at your bank or brokerage (e.g., E-Trade, etc.). Make sure to compare the fees. Lower fees are better. Just ask them for a form (or go online) to open the account.

For 529s, it's a little more involved. You need to make the following decisions:

- **Your state vs. other state plan:** There are ~100 different 529 plans. Each plan is attached to a state. For example, Georgia has the Path2College plan from TIAA-CREF. In 34 states, if you select your state's plan, you could be eligible for a state tax deduction on the amount you contribute.

But you are not required to get your state's plan. Most plans have no residency requirements. You can shop around. You can live in Georgia and buy a plan from Ohio. Another state's plan may have lower fees or better investment options. It's your choice. Go to saving-forcollege.com to compare plans.

- **Prepaid tuition 529 or College savings 529:** Every 529 plan is either a prepaid tuition plan or college savings plan. Here are the differences:

  o *Prepaid Tuition 529s:* With a prepaid tuition plan, you are pre-paying tuition at specific schools designated by the plan. You do not select any investments. They take care of everything and promise to pay in the future.

  For example, Florida's Prepaid College Plan covers a range of state colleges and universities in Florida. If your child does not attend the eligible school, the plan generally pays a set amount for any college. Each plan is different and for most of these plans you must be a resident of the state.

  o *College Savings 529s:* College savings 529 plans are simply college savings accounts. You select the investments. You can use the money for any accredited school. It's your choice.

You can't go wrong with either option.

If you like complete control and flexibility, select a college savings 529 plan. Just keep in mind that your investments could lose money.

If you're worried about college costs and investing, select a prepaid plan. Just remember, you have no control on the investments.

Either way, you're saving for college. That's a plus.

Taxes and 10%...
Don't use 529s and college savings money as your personal bank account. It's not an emergency fund. It doesn't serve multiple purposes. It's for education. And, there are rules to make sure that's the case.

If you use your college savings money for anything other than qualified educational expenses, you will pay taxes on the gains and a 10% penalty. For example, if your 529 plan has gained $5,000 and you withdraw it for a family vacation, you will pay taxes and a 10% penalty on the $5,000. If you're in the 25% tax bracket, you will owe $1,250 (25% x $5,000) in taxes and another $500 (10% x $500) in penalties. That's a $1,750 total bill for that year. I sure hope the vacation was memorable.

There are a few exceptions. If your child gets a scholarship and doesn't need the 529 savings, you will owe taxes but not the penalty. The same holds true if your child becomes disabled or dies.

Simply put, college savings money is for college (or, in the case of Coverdell plans, for K-12 or college). Don't use it for other stuff. If you don't have an emergency fund, have debt, or haven't saved for retirement, don't save for college. This is tank #6!

College 4: Select your investments

You've decided on a 529 or Coverdell plan. Now, you need to select the investments. Follow two simple rules of thumb.

1. Be more aggressive when your child is young. Get more conservative as your child gets closer to college.

If you have a 3-year-old, you have 15 years before they start college. You can take more risks so your money has a chance to grow. This means buying more equity or index mutual funds.

When your child is 16, college is right around the corner. You'll need the money in a few years. Invest more conservatively. This means buying more bonds or money market funds.

Fortunately, many college savings plans have options that follow this investment strategy for you. Funds called Year of Enrollment, Glide path, Age-Based, and Managed Allocation are designed to go from aggressive to conservative based on your child's age. There are tons of variations within these plans. They are not all alike. Do your research. Know how aggressive and how conservative they are. Even within the same age-based plan, there may be 4-5 different tracks. Take your time. Make a decision. Track the progress.

2. Avoid fees.

I don't like paying for anything. I especially hate overpaying. High fees can kill your investment returns. You saw it in the retirement section. The same holds true with 529 plans. Here are a few different fees you need to compare (and keep as low as possible):

- **Enrollment/application fee:** This is the fee to apply and enroll in the program. It's not common, but a few plans have these fees.

- **Account maintenance fee:** This is an annual fee to simply have the account. It usually gets waived with higher account balances. This is similar to a monthly fee on a checking account.

- **Asset management fees:** These fees pay the bank or brokerage firm to manage your money. You will always pay these fees but they can kill you if they're too high. A simple difference of .10% can have an impact of thousands of dollars.

- **Load and distribution fees:** You don't want to pay these fees. These fees pay the broker for selling you the 529 plan. You can buy direct from the specific plan you choose and avoid these fees. You don't need a broker. Simply call the plan, ask your questions, and make a decision.

When comparing plans, look at all the fees. Don't simply say, "I don't want to pay an application fee so I'm not choosing this one." That's crazy. Instead, add up all the fees and see how they would impact your investment over time.

Saving for college can be overwhelming. When your child is young, you want to do everything for them. When they're 15 and slamming doors, you feel like pulling the rug out from under them. Don't put too much pressure on yourself. If you've made it to tank #6, you're doing very well. Saving for college is the icing on the cake. Do what you can. Leave the rest to them.

Note

Tank #6 comes after #5. Save for your retirement first. Then, if you have more *fuel*, save for your children's college. It sounds selfish, but it's not. You can't borrow for retirement. Your kids can borrow for college. If it makes you feel better, write the following in your will:

"I, [enter your name], bequeath my assets to pay for the following. First, all outstanding student loans for my children. Second, college savings for my grandkids. Third, if anything is left over, [put whatever you want here]."

This way, you pay for their education without ever being dependent on them. Everyone wins.

◎ Carter Family: #6 - Children's College

John and Tina love little Willy. He's getting so big. They know he's gifted. They really should save for his college. But they haven't filled tank #5. They haven't put the full 20% of gross income to retirement. This plan says they shouldn't save for Willy's college yet. That's hard. It's particularly hard on Tina. Are they doing the right thing?

This is the part of the 7-Tank System where the Carter family can make trade-offs. The system says to fill tank #5 and put 20% of gross income toward retirement. But if Tina's losing sleep over it, she could put a little each month into a Coverdell or 529 for Willy. She's buying peace of mind. That's fantastic. Sure, it doesn't exactly follow the system, but the system is a compass, not the law. She understands the trade-off and decides on the following:

- After they fill tank #4, Tina will contribute $50/month to a Coverdell plan for Willy. It means a little less going to retirement. She's okay with that. John's happy that she's happy. Smart man.

- John and Tina update their will to state, "We, John and Tina Carter, bequeath our assets to pay for the following. First, all outstanding student loans for our children. Second, college savings for my grandchildren.....etc." (Get a qualified attorney to write the exact legal language).

If John and Tina continue to have *financial fuel* each month and work through the steps, plenty of money will go to Willy.

#7 - Bucket List

You made it! The last tank. You've got a full emergency fund. You're debt-free. You're saving 20% for retirement. You may be putting aside money for your kid's college education. You feel good about yourself. Now, go on a spending spree so you end up back where you started. Hahaha...just kidding.

Tank #7 is about you. It's about ticking through your bucket list with your money. Vacations, a new Harley, floor seats to an Atlanta Hawks game, money to start a business, down payment on a new home, paying off your not-so-bad debt, a personal cook, the list goes on.

But wait, I know what you're thinking.

"It will take me years to fill tanks 1-6! I can't do anything for myself until then? I can't even save for a house. Forget that!"

Good point. That doesn't make sense. It's not realistic. Tank #7 should be part of the entire process. It is.

If you want to do anything that fits in tank #7 before filling the rest, try the following:

- **Reduce spending:** The best way to find money for your bucket list while filling the other tanks is to cut your spending. If you want to take a vacation, cut the amount you spend on clothes. If you want a new car, stop eating out. Make trade-offs in your spending. Keep the same amount of *fuel*. Fill the tanks with the same timeline.

- **Increase income:** Can't find anywhere to cut? Make more money. If you truly want to take that vacation, you'll take the time and effort to generate side income. Reread the section on "Getting More *Fuel*."

- **Lower your fuel:** I don't like this option, but it's still an option. You can add "savings for a down payment" to your budget and reduce the amount of *fuel* you put towards your next tank. Just remember, it will take you longer to fill all the tanks. Too many of these and you may not finish at all.

- **Don't do it:** I like this option. Sure, you need a break every so often, but you don't need a trip every 2 months. Say 'no' more than you say 'yes'. Focus on getting through the sysstem.

Ultimately, you want to fill tanks 1-6 as quickly as possible.

Once you fill tanks #1-4, you're stable.

After tank #5, you're free.

Tank #6 is icing on the cake.

And tank #7 is eating the whole cake.

The cake tastes much better after you've filled all the tanks. But I understand if you need a little taste every so often.

Saving on Your Bucket List

No point in paying full price for your bucket list, right? Here are some more specific savings tips on some common bucket list items.

Flights
Airlines are constantly reinventing their fares. They're trying to stay profitable. On some carriers, you pay a super-low fare for the flight and then get charged for everything else. Other airlines have higher fares but include peanuts. Here are a few ways to save on flights.

- **Consolidator sites:** The following sites will compare airlines and fares. They're all about the same. Most don't include some discount airlines such as Southwest (so you'll need to check those airlines separately).

  o Kayak.com
  o Orbitz.com
  o Expedia.com
  o Getgoing.com
  o Hipmunk.com
  o Southwest.com
  o Priceline.com
  o Yapta.com (to track fares)
  o Airfarewatchdog.com (to track fares)

  Every airline has different fare classes and dynamic pricing based on supply and demand. Focus on finding the fare that fits your budget instead of holding out for the lowest fare or some unreasonable number.

- **Buy on weekdays:** Buy your tickets on a Tuesday or Wednesday. Often, new, lower fare classes are introduced on these days. In addition, there are fewer people buying so you may get some great rates.

- **Travel on weekdays:** Middle-of-the-week travel saves you money. If you have flexibility, travel on a Wednesday and Saturday to save.

- **Travel light:** Fit your stuff in a carry-on. Don't worry, your smile is far more attractive than those extra shoes you want to pack. Avoid paying baggage fees.

- **Drive:** Yes, if you have a family of 4, driving will always be cheaper. There are plenty of awesome adventures within a 4-6 hour drive.

Lodging

Hotels are no longer the only option. Here are ways to save on lodging:

- **Vacation rentals:** The world of vacation rentals has exploded. You can literally rent someone's apartment for the weekend at half the cost of the hotel next door. You can even rent out your place (see "Making More Money"). It's all legit and can save you hundreds or thousands. Here are a few sites to get started:

  - Airbnb.com
  - Vrbo.com
  - Homeaway.com

- **Points:** Got hotel points? Use them. Programs such as Starwood Preferred Guest will let you combine cash and points to save on great hotels.

- **Name your price:** If you want a location and star rating but don't care about the brand, try "naming your price" at Priceline.com. The downside is you can't cancel and they charge you immediately, but you can get some amazing deals.

- **Consolidator sites:** Most of the sites we've just mentioned for flights can also help you find hotel deals.

Transportation

Do you really need to rent a car? Maybe not. Here's how you can cut your transportation bill on vacations:

- **Ride sharing:** Uber and Lyft are the largest ride-sharing services. Download the app. You will save up to 30% vs. local taxis.

- **Public transport:** Most big cities have amazing public transportation. Use it. It saves on car rental fees and parking.

- **Consolidator sites:** Most of the sites we mentioned for flight can also help you find rental car deals. Check if your credit card provides insurance coverage. Then, deny their coverage. Remember, renting a car also means parking, gas, and tolls. Think about the total cost of renting before making the decision.

Personal Assistant

How about your own cook? Maybe your own driver? That's only for rich people, right? Not anymore. Wealth is about owning your time. The following sites can get you some of your time back:

- **Ride sharing:** As we just noted, Uber and Lyft are the largest ride sharing services. It's like having your own personal driver. Download the app. You can save up to 30% vs. local taxis.

- **Prepared meals:** Blueapron.com, Plated.com and HelloFresh.com send you ingredients to prepare great meals. They take the thinking out of cooking. Home-Bistro.com and Freshandfitcuisine.com send you the entire meal. If done correctly, you can actually save money using these services.

- **Virtual assistant:** Yes, your own personal assistant. Well, actually it's a virtual assistant. They can do everything from researching daycares to setting up travel to helping you keep a family calendar. Companies such as Zirtual.com and Upwork.com make it easy to find an assistant.

Buying a Home

This isn't a book about buying a home. That being said, homeownership is a bucket list item for many people. Notice, I didn't say it was a necessity. If you're considering buying a home, make sure you can say 'yes' to the following four questions:

- Do you have a 1-month emergency fund and little-to-no bad debt?

- In addition to the above, do you have enough cash to put 10% down? Do not include pulling from your 401(k).

- Can you buy in a good, stable location? Areas with great elementary schools tend to hold their value.

- Are you planning on staying in the house for at least five years?

Don't be house poor. Make sure you're ready to buy. The best case scenario would be to buy after you've filled tank #4. If you want to do it before, tread lightly.

Paying Off Your Home Early

If you already own a home, paying it off early can be a great bucket list item. The three most common ways to pay off a mortgage are:

1. Adding extra money to your payment every month.
2. Shifting to biweekly payments.
3. Adding a lump sum payment such as a bonus or tax refund when possible.

I'll use the Carter family to illustrate the impact of each option.

John and Tina bought a home two years ago with the following terms:

- **Mortgage amount**: $250,000
- **Type**: 30-year fixed mortgage
- **Interest rate:** 4.5%
- **Principal and interest payment:** $1,267 *(excluding taxes and insurance because they won't change)*

Today, they have $241,749 left of their mortgage. They've made payments for 2 years and have another 28 years left.

Once they reach tank #7, they decide they want to pay off their home. They can download a great Excel home mortgage calculator at vertex42.com/Calculators/home-mortgage-calculator.html to evaluate different options.

Here's the impact of the three most common ways to pay off a mortgage compared to simply continuing their current payments.

Mortgage Payoff Options

Option	Description	Years to pay	Interest saved
Continue current payments	They keep doing what they're doing.	28	None
1) Pay an extra $100 per month	They decide to add a $100 more to each payment. They must designate this additional amount as principal.	24 years, 3 months	~$28,100
2) Make biweekly payments	Instead of paying the mortgage each month, John and Tina could pay half the mortgage every 2 weeks. The principal and interest payment would be $633.50 ($1,267/2) every 2 weeks. They would make this payment twenty-six times throughout the year. That's equivalent of making one extra monthly payment each year.	24 years, 1 month	~$30,100
3) Apply bonus or lump-sum cash to mortgage	John and Tina may have unpredictable income. They can apply some of their bonus or commission checks to pay down the mortgage.	Varies	Varies

Paying off your home is a financial and emotional decision. I understand that you may have a personal desire to own your home outright. That's fantastic. It shows you hate debt. But, don't make it a priority until you've paid off bad debt, stocked your emergency fund, and are contributing 20% of your gross income to retirement.

Starting a Business

"Boss." Sounds good, but it's not nearly as glamorous as you might think. Starting a business is risky. It's unpredictable. It can be emotional. It could mean a serious downside to your money. But what's life without a dream? If you're thinking about starting your own business, take the following steps to save you time and money:

- **Customer discovery:** Call twenty potential customers. Ask questions. Learn their pain points. Don't try to sell them. Build the relationship. This should not cost you anything except your time.

- **Know the competitors:** Your idea is not new. Find the competitors. How are they structured? How are you different? Should you work with a competitor first?

- **Fail fast:** If it's not working, stop. Sure, you need to be persistent, but be honest with yourself. Change directions. Don't add more money and time if it's not working. You will ultimately succeed.

I'm sure I've left hundreds of items off this list, but I hope it helps you get started. Tank #7 is about eating the whole cake. It's about making your dreams a reality. When you get here, time is your only enemy. Use it wisely.

◎ Carter Family: #7 - Bucket List

Incorporating tank #7 as you work through the rest of the system is an art, not a science. John and Tina are working through the tanks and haven't reached #7. Does that mean they can't take vacations or attend a wedding or do a little skydiving? No, not at all. That's unrealistic. It will drive them crazy.

Instead, John and Tina must make trade-offs. Here's what they decided to do:

- **Vacations:** The Carters decided to take two vacations a year — one in the summer and one during the Christmas holidays. They will drive somewhere near-by. They will rent a place using airbnb.com. They will cook most of their meals. They expect each trip to cost $800-$1,000. It's possible.

- **Meal Delivery:** With two full-time jobs, cooking is hard. It's stressful. They picked a meal delivery service for three days/week. They cook on the weekends.

That's it. That's where they're starting. To offset the costs, they're cutting some monthly entertainment/clothes purchases and Tina's working overtime. Exhibit 8 shows the Carter family's final revised budget.

They both see the path. It takes time. They're willing to make the trade-offs and hold each other accountable. Soon, they'll have plenty of money to spend more on their bucket list. It's a journey.

Exhibit 8: Carter family budget, <u>final</u>

INCOME	
Take home pay	
John	$ 3,320
Tina	$ 2,390
Extra Cash	
Selling stuff and overtime	$ 250
TOTAL TAKE HOME PAY	**$ 5,960**
EXPENSES	
Housing/Car	
Mortgage	$ 1,650
Car note (John)	$ 350
Utilities	
Electric	$ 130
Gas	$ 90
Water (occurs every 3 months)	$ 50
TV/Internet	$ 190
Cellphone	$ 140
Insurance	
Auto	$ 175
Debt	
Student loans	$ 300
Credit cards (minimum payments)	$ 100
Other debt minimum payments	$ 200
Personal Expenses	
Willy's daycare	$ 800
Groceries	$ 475
Eating out	$ 215
Entertainment	$ 75
Clothes/shoes	$ 60
Tithe	$ 200
Gas for the cars	$ 300
Medical copays/prescriptions	$ 100
Personal items	$ 50
Vacation savings	$ 160
TOTAL EXPENSES	**$ 5,810**
FINANCIAL FUEL	**$ 150**

Summary of the 7-Tank System

Remember, it all starts with the most important number in your financial life - *financial fuel*. That's the amount of money you spend less than you make every month. You must track it. If you don't have *fuel*, focus all your efforts on getting *fuel*. Once you have *fuel*, you can fill tanks in the 7-Tank System.

Here's a summary of the 7 tanks:

Tank	Name	Description
1	Company Match for Retirement	If your employer matches retirement contributions, take advantage. It's free money. It will reduce your income today but can yield thousands in the future.
2	1-Month Emergency Fund	If you lost your job, how much money do you need to survive for a month? That's your 1-month emergency fund. Build this fund as fast as possible so you have a safety net.
3	Bad Debt Free	Bad debt includes mob debt, credit cards, private student loans, tax debt, 401(K) loans and other high interest debt. Pay these off as soon as possible.
4	Emergency Fund to cover 3-6 Months	You're out of debt and have a little cash in the bank. Don't get lazy. Grow your emergency fund to cover 3-6 months of expenses.
5	20% of Gross Income to Retirement	You've addressed all short-term needs. Now it's time to get serious about the long term. Put 20% of your gross income to retirement.
6	Children's College	If you have *financial fuel* after saving 20% towards retirement, you can begin saving for your children's college. Don't feel obligated to pay for all their expenses. They should have some skin in the game.
7	Bucket List	It's time to seize the day. In reality, you'll live your bucket list throughout the 7-steps. Just remember to balance these 'wants' while working through the system.

◎ The Carter Family Filling 7-Tanks

The Carter family is working their way through the 7 tanks. It's not easy. John and Tina are newlyweds with a rambunctious 2-year old. Life is busy. Fortunately, the 7-Tank System gave them a guide to get on the same page and get focused.

Exhibit 9 gives an overview of how the Carter family plans to fill the 7 tanks and expected timeline. This is the biggest part of their financial plan. It doesn't need a fancy binder or annoying buzz words. It just requires a commitment to monthly *financial fuel* and a timeline. The more *fuel* they get, the faster they'll fill the tanks. If they keep having less *fuel* each month, it could take forever.

Everyone's timeline will look different but one truth remains the same. The more *fuel* you get, the faster you go. With less *fuel*, it will take longer. The ball's in your court. You decide.

Exhibit 9: Carter family timeline

Tank	Name	Carter family	Amount	Estimated time
1	Company Match for Retirement	John's employer matches up to 5% so he contributes 5%. Tina's employer doesn't match.	5%	Immediately
2	1-Month Emergency Fund	$3,000 will get them through one month. They have $600 and need an additional $2,400. With $150 of monthly *financial fuel*, this step will take ~16 months.	$3,000	16 months
3	Bad Debt Free	They have ~$15,000 of bad debt. As they pay off each debt, they will add that payment to the next. This step will take them ~33 months.	$15,000	33 months
4	Emergency Fund to cover 3-6 Months	They decide a 4-month fund ($12,000) will be sufficient. They need to save an addition $9,000. With no bad debt payments, they will have over $600 of *fuel*. This step will take ~15 months.	Additional $9,000	15 months
5	20% of Gross Income to Retirement	John will already be contributing 5% in step #1. His employer will add 2.5%. Therefore, he will add another 12.5% to retirement. Tina will work towards contributing the full 20%. John will use his employer's 401(k) while Tina will open an IRA.	20% of gross income	Until retirement
6	Children's College	Tina can't sleep unless she's saving for Willy's college. She knows step #6 comes after step #5 but this is about peace of mind. After step #4, she will add $50/month to Willy's 529 plan.	At their discretion	Through college
7	Bucket List	John and Tina need to keep their sanity and motivation through the process. They've decided to take two vacations each year and start getting meals delivered. It's part of their journey.	At their discretion	Throughout the 7-step journey

Parting Shots

The Ups and Downs of *Financial Fuel*

Stay Accountable

Set Realistic Expectations

Enjoy the Journey

The Ups and Downs of *Financial Fuel*

For nearly a decade, I helped major companies craft their business strategies. The most successful companies stuck to their strategy through thick and thin. Sure, there were adjustments along the way, but the core strategy stayed constant. In the face of adversity, the successful companies did not abandon their plan. Instead, they doubled down. The same holds true for you and your financial plan.

Your timeline to get through the 7-Tank System assumes you get the same amount of *fuel* each month. It's predictable. Unfortunately, life is not predictable. You'll have ups and downs. Some months you'll have more *fuel* than you imagined. Other months will feel like one big emergency. It's okay. Don't panic. In fact, the next few pages will show you how *financial fuel* generally varies over the course of a year and your life.

Fuel in a Year

Assume you're targeting $300 of *fuel* per month. It won't be the same every month. It's hard to save during the summers and holidays. Make up for it during the fall and spring. Don't fight the natural tide. Just make sure you're averaging $300. Here's how your *fuel* may look over the course of a year if your goal is to average $300/month:

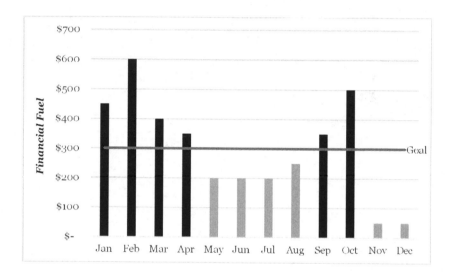

Fuel in a Lifetime

These same ups and downs happen throughout your life. You'll get more *fuel* as DINKS (double income no kids) than when you have two kids in daycare and a new home. Stockpile *fuel* when you can. Save as if you'll never earn again. Accept the times when you can't. Keep your head above water. Here's a look at the highs and lows of *fuel* during your life:

Life stage	Expected *Fuel*
Single	Medium
DINKS	High
Kids/homeowner	Low
School aged kids	Low/Medium
Empty nesters	High
Retirement	Medium

Fuel varies throughout a year and a lifetime. Understand it. Accept it. Roll with it.

Stay Accountable

You can quit. No one will know. Your friends won't say anything. Companies will be happy. You can justify it to yourself. It's easy.

Staying accountable, on the other hand, is hard. It's especially hard when you're $300 over budget and there's still a week left in the month. You're simply trying to stop the bleeding and you're tapped out of determination and willpower.

These times will happen along you're journey. They will happen more than once. I hope you can weather the storm. I hope you don't quit. Here are a few tips that will help:

- **Find a partner:** Find a person (or couple) that will constantly annoy you to stay on track. Tell them your goals and give them permission to ask for updates. Compete with them. Set regular check-ins. You don't need to share your finances. Instead, they're that extra voice to help you stay accountable. Ideally, that voice is annoying enough that you stay on track to get them off your back.

- **Set shorter goals and use cash:** Staying on track for a month may feel like an eternity. Instead, set a mini-budget for the weekend. Take cash out on Friday. Don't carry your credit cards. Make the cash last until Monday morning. Do it again next weekend.

- **Pay yourself first:** Calculate how much *fuel* you expect to save this month and put it in a savings account at the beginning of the month. Now, you can spend whatever is left in your checking account. This strategy does not replace a budget. Instead, it helps you avoid temptation because your *fuel* is no longer in your checking account.

- **Set daily reminders:** Remind yourself to track every day. Set a daily alarm on your phone. Put a post it note on your bathroom mirror. Setup an automated daily email to yourself that says, "Track your s***." Figure out what works for you. Keep poking yourself.

- **Get rewards:** Reward yourself after tracking for one month. Reward yourself after filling a tank. Reward yourself for a record month of financial *fuel*. Be generous with your rewards along the journey.

- **Tell anyone who will listen:** Tell others about your quest to get on track with your money. Share tips. Offer support. Become the billboard for making good financial choices. You'll create positive peer pressure to do what you say.

Again, staying accountable is hard. There will be multiple opportunities to quit. Try to involve others as much as possible. Be open about your journey. Don't go at this alone.

Set Realistic Expectations

I have a friend who is late to everything. If the dinner starts at 8pm, he'll show up at 9:30. If we're meeting for coffee at 2pm, he'll get there at 3. Even if I lie and tell him the 8pm dinner is at 7:30, he'll still show up an hour late. For years, I would get frustrated. Let me rephrase that – for years, I would get pissed. I would appeal to him and others about how disrespectful it was to always show up late. Then, after nearly a decade, my wife asked a simple question, "Why do you expect him to show up on time?" I didn't have an answer. She was right. My frustrations were less about him and more about my own, unrealistic expectations. Every time I expected him to be on time, I was setting myself up for failure.

As you plan your journey, don't set unrealistic expectations. Don't let your excitement cloud your judgement. You will not pay off all your debt in a few months. You will not have positive *fuel* every month. You're new business idea will not go viral overnight. All these goals take time. Your job is to set a timeline that will push you, but is realistic.

For most people starting at tank #1, completing tank #4 will take three to five years. If you've already filled a few tanks, it will take less time. If you're still working on getting positive *financial fuel*, it could take longer. Regardless of where you are, focus on the tank you're on. Focus on tracking your money every day. Focus on making good decisions.

Bill Gates once said, "We overestimate what we can do in a day and underestimate what we can achieve in a year." He's absolutely right. Set realistic expectations and, over time, you'll surprise yourself.

Enjoy the Journey

You spend 70-80% of your take home pay. If you bring home $4,000/month and want $500 of *financial fuel*, you will spend $3,500. That's three thousand five hundred dollars you get to spend. Enjoy it.

If your budget includes a night out for dinner, chow down. If your budget includes a car payment for a great ride, drive it with the top down. Even if your budget includes a pair of shoes to add to a collection that you never wear, more power to you. What you do with the amount you can spend is up to you. The worst thing you can do is forget to enjoy it.

Now I know what you're saying: "My spending money barely pays my bills. I'm always behind." Got it. Change your bills. If you want to go out more, get a cheaper car. If you need to upgrade the wardrobe, stop eating out as much. If you're stressed and need a vacation, maybe it's time to give up that expensive iPhone plan. And, if you can't find places to cut, re-read the "Making More Money" section of this book, pick a strategy, get off your ass, and get started. You have complete control over your *financial fuel*. Some changes may take time, but they're all possible. Just remember, once it's part of your budget, **enjoy it**.

Worksheets

Completing the following worksheets will help you get organized and begin your journey through the 7-Tank System.

Tracking Your *Fuel*

The following worksheets will help you assess your current *financial fuel*.

Tracking

1. How do you track your budget to know how much *financial fuel* you have each month?

    ☐ Mobile App.
    ☐ Website / Online tool.
    ☐ Excel.
    ☐ Pen / Pad.
    ☐ Abacus.
    ☐ In my head...which doesn't always work.
    ☐ **I don't** and promise to start.

2. My next step for tracking my budget is _ _ _ _ _ _ _ _ _ _

_ _

My *Financial Fuel*
How much *fuel* did you have over the past three months? (Go to pages 14-15 to learn how to calculate your *fuel*)

Month	Income	Expenses	*Financial Fuel*

Your Budget

To succeed in this system, you need a budget. Fill in the template below with your categories and amounts and see if you're on the path to positive *financial fuel*.

INCOME	
After tax income	
You	
Spouse	
Extra cash	
Some type of extra income	
TOTAL TAKE HOME PAY	$ -
EXPENSES	
Housing/Car	
Rent / mortgage	
Car note(s)	
Utilities	
Electric, gas, water	
TV, Internet, Cellphone	
Insurance	
Auto, Life, etc.	
Debt	
Student loans	
Credit cards (min payments)	
Other debt min payments	
Personal expenses	
Groceries	
Eating out / entertainment	
Gas for the cars	
Clothes/shoes	
Medical copays/prescriptions	
Cash	
TOTAL EXPENSES	$ -
FINANCIAL FUEL	$ -

Getting More *Fuel*

There are only two ways to get more fuel – make more or spend less. Write down specific ideas on how you plan to do each. (Refer to pages 30-48 for ideas)

Make more

Idea	Amount	Next Steps

Spend less

Idea	Amount	Next Steps

7 Tanks to Fill with Your *Fuel*

Use the following worksheets to get organized and identify where you are in the 7-Tank System.

#1 - Company Match for Retirement

Does your employer offer a retirement match? If so, how much is it?

You	Spouse
☐ Yes. How Much? _____%	☐ Yes. How Much? _____%
☐ No.	☐ No.
☐ I don't know but will ask.	☐ I don't know but will ask.

#2 - 1-month Emergency Fund

How much money would you need to cover expenses for one month if you and your spouse lost your jobs? (e.g., core expenses include rent/mortgage, minimum loan payments, food, etc. – the bare minimums).

$

#3 - Bad Debt Free

The first step of paying off debt is knowing what you owe. Fill in the tables below to get organized.

Bad debt (includes credit cards, tax debt, medical debt, private student loans, 401(k) / retirement plan loans, payday loans, title loans, and other high interest debt)

Type of Bad Debt	Date	Initial Amount	Interest Rate	Min Pmt	Current Balance
Total bad debt		$ -		$ -	$ -

Not-so-bad debt (includes federal student loans, auto loans, mortgage and home equity)

Type of Not-so-bad Debt	Date	Initial Amount	Interest Rate	Min Pmt	Current Balance
Total not-so-bad debt		$ -		$ -	$ -

#4 - Emergency Fund to Cover 3-6 Months

Once your bad debt is paid off, it's time to build serious cushion in your emergency fund. Use the table below to calculate how much you need to fill tank #4.

	Amount
Enter amount from tank #2 for your 1-month emergency fund	
Enter total number of additional months you want for your full emergency fund (must be >3)	x
Amount you need to fill tank #4	

#5 - 20% of Gross Income to Retirement

When you reach tank #5, you're free. Now let's figure out how much you need to save to make sure you don't run out of money.

Retirement 1: Social Security and pension

Set up an account at ssa.gov/myaccount to get your estimated social security benefit. Enter the information below.

When it's taken	You	Spouse
At full retirement age (67)		
At age 70		
At early retirement age (62)		

In addition, if you have any pensions, list them below with the estimated monthly payment. If your pension is a lump sum, do not enter it here.

Pension from...	Estimated Monthly Amount[1]

[1] *If your pension payout is a lump sum, do not enter it here. Instead, enter it as part of retirement savings in 'retirement 3'*

Retirement 2: Calculate "Your Retirement Number"

Now, let's calculate how much you'll need at retirement.

Step	Amount
Enter current gross annual combined household income	$
x % of income you will need in retirement	*x 75%*
= How much you need each year in retirement	=
- expected annual social security[1]	-
- expected annual pensions	-
= How much your savings needs to provide each year	=
x by 25	*x 25*
= Amount you need to save before retirement	=
x by inflation factor (see table)	x
Your Retirement Number	=

[1] *Multiply your expected __monthly__ social security at age 67 by 12 to get your estimated __annual__ social security. If it's you and your spouse, add both.*

Inflation Table (for calculating "Your Retirement Number")

Years to Retirement	Inflation Factor
10	1.34
15	1.56
20	1.81
25	2.09
30	2.43
35	2.81
40	3.26
45	3.78

Retirement 3: Calculate monthly savings to reach 'Your Retirement Number'

Now, let's calculate how much you'll need to save each month to reach "Your Retirement Number". Plug in your numbers as follows into the online calculator located at:

www.bankrate.com/calculators/savings/saving-goals-calculator.aspx

Question on bankrate calculator	Answer
How much do you want to save?	Enter "Your Retirement Number"
How many years do you have in which to save it?	Enter [67 - your age]
What interest rate do you expect to earn on your savings?	5%
Compounding	Monthly
How much money can you spare for your first deposit?	Enter your current retirement balance
Do you wish to skip savings 2 weeks each year?	No
Date of first deposit	Enter current date
Amount you need to save monthly	=

The amount you calculated in the table above is your goal. It includes any match you receive from your employer. Remember, it won't happen overnight.

Retirement 4: Decide where to save it

Your final step is selecting investments. A few key decisions you will need to make include:

- Roth vs. Traditional accounts
- Using your employer's plan vs. opening an IRA
- Selecting specific mutual funds and ensuring your risk level is appropriate for your age

Refer to pages 101-108 to understand your options.

#6- Children's College

If you have monthly *fuel* after filling tank #5, you can start saving for your children's college. Let's calculate how much you will need to save each month to pay for their school.

Step	Amount
Enter estimated cost of 1 year of college	$
x Cost factor (see table)	x
= Estimated future cost of 1 year of college	=
x Years in college	x
= Estimated total college cost	=
x Savings factor (see table)	x
Required monthly savings	=

Cost and savings factor table

Years Until College	Cost Factor	Savings Factor
1	1.06	0.0814
2	1.12	0.0397
3	1.19	0.0258
4	1.26	0.0189
5	1.34	0.0147
6	1.42	0.0199
7	1.50	0.01
8	1.59	0.0085
9	1.69	0.0074
10	1.79	0.0064
11	1.90	0.0057
12	2.01	0.0051
13	2.13	0.0046
14	2.26	0.0041
15	2.40	0.0037
16	2.54	0.0034
17	2.69	0.0031
18	2.85	0.0029

Remember, there are multiple ways to pay for college including contributions from your child. Decide on a comfortable level to fill tank #6 and use either a 529 or Coverdell account to take advantage of the tax benefits.

#7- Bucket List

Ahh...you thought it would never come. Well, it's here – your bucket list. Right down your list below. Update it as often as you want. Check off items you complete. Keep calm and live life to the fullest!

Description	Estimated Cost

About the Author

In 2010, at the trough of the recession, Alok Deshpande, CEO and founder of SmartPath, left a distinguished consulting career to teach personal finance. In his mind, it was a simple decision,

> *"I wanted to make a direct impact on the people that I grew up around. Very few of them had ever been taught how to be smart with their money. And, I saw firsthand how painful the recession was to them."*

He started with a Saturday morning makeshift class with six students.

> *"We spent nearly four hours together going through just about every topic on money. They loved it and I knew I was on to something special."*

Six students became twenty, then fifty, then a hundred, and growth continued. Today, SmartPath teaches thousands of individuals and families every year through financial wellness programs and one on one coaching.

> *"It's been a dream come true to play a small part of moving people from chaos to confidence with their finances."*

Prior to starting SmartPath, Alok was a Manager at Bain & Company, a premier global managing consulting company. In that role, he served as an advisor to the C-Suite of Fortune 500 companies on a range of topics including corporate strategy, mergers and acquisitions, human capital, and new market opportunities.

Alok received a BBA with high distinction from Emory's Goizueta Business School and an MBA from Harvard Business School. In addition, Alok is a member of Leadership Atlanta and stays active in his local community through volunteering and nonprofit Board positions. He resides in Atlanta, Georgia with his wife and son.

For more information about SmartPath financial education programs or to book Alok Deshpande as a speaker, please send a request to:

info@smartpathfinancial.com